*Trevor Beeson*

# An Eye for an Ear

**SCM PRESS LTD**

334  00434  9

*First published 1972*
*by SCM Press Ltd*
*56 Bloomsbury Street London*

© *SCM Press Ltd 1972*

*Printed in Great Britain by*
*Richard Clay (The Chaucer Press) Ltd*
*Bungay, Suffolk*

*scm centrebooks · christian casebooks*

*already published*

Managing the Church / *W. E. Beveridge*
The Casework Ministry / *Joan B. Miller*
Case Studies in Unity / *R. M. C. Jeffery*
The Christian in Education / *Colin Alves*
An Eye for an Ear / *Trevor Beeson*

*in preparation*

Solitary Refinement / *Sister Madeleine* OSA

# Contents

1  The Nature of Communication                     7

2  What is There to Communicate?                  20

3  Across the Centuries                           29

4  The Written Word                               51

5  The Spoken Word                                70

6  The Visual Word                                86

7  The Church is the Message                     107

# Contents

1. 
2. 
3. 
4. 
5. 
6. 
7.

# 1   The Nature of Communication

Shortly before leaving the staff of St Martin-in-the-Fields in 1971, I ventured once again into the pulpit of that famous church. Although the 'occasional' preacher often finds it difficult to attune to the unique St Martin's wavelength, those who have been privileged to be on the church's staff for a number of years know that it is one of the easiest places in the world in which to deliver a sermon. Architecturally, the building was designed for the purpose. In a country where church attendance is declining rapidly, the St Martin's congregations – composed of people from many parts of the world and ranging from prime ministers to paupers – are still large. Moreover, they come to the church *expecting* the preacher to have something interesting and relevant to say, and many are prepared to tell him afterwards whether or not he has spoken to their condition.

On this particular Sunday morning, I felt moved to preach on the well-known Pauline text from Galatians: 'Christ set us free to be free men'. The main theme of the sermon was Jesus the liberator – the man who came to set men free from all that enslaves them, politically, socially, economically, psychologically, sexually and racially. The church (the community of Jesus) was portrayed as a society placed in the world as the embodiment of and agency for freedom. The theological basis of the sermon was presented in terms of the remembrance of the Jesus of the past, the awareness of his liberating power in the present, and the hope of that deliverance which he promised at the end of time. All carefully worked out and reasonably coherent.

At the end of the service a very tall, distinguished-looking member of the congregation shook me by the hand and declared the sermon to be the best and most helpful he had ever heard. His only regret was the worship surrounding the sermon did not attain the same high level. As one who believes that Christian worship should itself be a communication of the gospel, and that a very considerable amount of reform is required in most places before it becomes so, I warmed to this comment. But there was no time to discuss it further in the draughty portico of the church in Trafalgar Square, so the impressive gentleman promised me a letter on the subject. Within a few days the letter arrived from the Army and Navy Club. Its signature was that of a naval commander who is a member of one of Scotland's aristocratic families. Again the virtues of the sermon were extolled, but then came the suggestions for adjusting the worship to accord more closely with the spoken message. 'You should not allow that black man to carry the cross at the head of the choir procession. You should sing the National Anthem at the close of the service.' Clearly, the requirements of his liturgical revolution were simple, but far-reaching.

This incident seems worth mentioning on the opening pages of a book on the subject of Christian communication if only to emphasize as strongly as possible that, even in one of the most favourable settings, the church has a major problem on its hands when it relies on traditional methods of communication. It will also serve as a warning that the author is ill-equipped for the offering of answers – simple or complicated – to the greatest problem now facing the Christian community: 'How do we share what we have learned of Christ with those who have not yet entered into the Christian experience?' There are in fact no experts in this field; only a growing number of Christians who are aware that many of the traditional means of communication are no longer effective and are searching for something to take their place. I count myself among these seekers.

Amid the confusion, uncertainty and perplexity, one factor is however as clear as crystal: the Christian gospel demands that its adherents should share their experience with others. The gift of Christ is not a treasure to be hoarded by the individuals who receive it, for their own exclusive edification or comfort, but is to be shared and handed on to those other members of the human race who are able to accept it. There is a universal instinct which drives us to share what we most value with others, and in the case of the Christian faith there is a further imperative which springs from the fact that our own reception of the gospel is traceable to the readiness of individuals or the community of Christ to introduce us to the Jesus of the gospels and to the Jesus of contemporary experience and encounter.

This raises at once a fundamental question concerning motivation. Why do Christians wish to share their experience with others? In Western Europe, where the rapid growth of secularization is leading to a dramatic falling away from church membership, it is possible to discern a number of motives which seem to spring from a deeply-rooted sense of ecclesiastical insecurity and are ultimately attributable to lack of faith.

It must be freely admitted that it is less than comfortable to belong to a declining community, and that it can be exceedingly depressing to worship in a building where the congregation occupies less than one-tenth of the available seating. Church administrators are also well aware of the difficulties involved in the maintenance of a machinery designed by and for a fairly large number of people, but which is now used by small and widely scattered groups. Since the modification of the Christian community's arrangements – at both local and national levels – calls for a high degree of courage and effort, and since retrenchment seems to suggest failure, it is not altogether surprising if 'calls to mission' are offered as the most positive way forward. Stirring words from episcopal and moderatorial lips suggest that, given the will and the means, those empty pews can once again be filled and the accounts comfortably balanced. Never lacking is a number of clerics and congregations who can be held up as examples of what can be achieved when drive and imagination are effectively combined. The emphasis here is on recruitment and the parallels with the activities of provincial cinema managers and area sales representatives are obvious enough.

Few Christian leaders or church members are, however, prepared to speak in such crude terms – even though their actions frequently belie their words. Most frequently the 'call to mission' is couched in the language of assisting the heathen, or the immoral or the frustrated or the unhappy multitudes towards the discovery of life's secret. The world outside the church is discerned as hell-bent to destruction, and the Christian community must therefore do everything possible to halt this spectacular slide down the Gadarene slope. Once again, anxiety appears as the primary motivation of mission. At all costs individuals and society must be 'saved' from the consequences of disbelief. The Christian gospel offers the antidote to man's destructive propensity; it must, therefore, be applied speedily and with the utmost vigour – while there is yet time.

Motivations of this sort are easily recognizable from the techniques employed to secure the desired result. They are essentially propagandist. At one extreme the church develops a theology and discipline in which there is overwhelming emphasis on rewards and punishment. In mediaeval England and in those parts of the world where church and community are still inextricably woven together this technique offered, and still offers, a certain amount of success. If individuals and communities can be persuaded to believe that rejection of the Christian faith is certain to lead to the pains of hell, while its acceptance guarantees the sublime joys of heaven, there is a good chance that a fairly considerable number will 'sign on' for Christ and put in an appearance at Mass on Sundays. Buttressing by the discipline of confession and absolution, and the acceptance of an authoritarian form of priesthood will improve these chances.

At the other extreme is the mass meeting or crusade of which, historically, John Wesley was the prime exponent and Billy Graham is the latest in the succession. Here, with varying degrees of sophistication, the individual is subjected to powerful elements of suggestion, of which the most common manifestations are to be seen in 'heart-tugging' music, appeals to the guilt feelings of the audience and a carefully organized 'response' to the appeal of the preacher designed to ensure that those who do not stand up to be counted as converts are made to feel members of an awkward, unredeemed minority. Well arranged follow-up classes and courses of instruction will, it is hoped, reduce the losses which are inevitable when decisions have been made in a state of high emotion or under extreme pressure. Again, there is considerable emphasis on rewards and punishment. The preacher does not hesitate to use stories in which well-known personalities met sudden death in a motoring accident, without having first taken the precaution of committing themselves to Christ, or in which a successful business man found even greater success after accepting the cross as his trademark.

It must be emphasized that these are extreme, even if not uncommon, examples of techniques designed to communicate the Christian gospel to those who have not yet accepted it. Between the extremes are a multitude of variations on similar themes, each of which will, it is hoped, have the desired effect of confronting individuals with Christ and thus bringing them into the society which bears his name and is committed to the extension of his kingdom. This is what the church normally understands by Christian communication and if any questions are raised about the subject they are invariably concerned with the efficiency or otherwise of the techniques employed and not with their fundamental motivation and integrity.

The similarity between these techniques and those of Goebbels and other notorious propagandists is not altogether superficial. They share common ground inasmuch as they are designed to bring about a change of mind or attitude in an individual through the application of pressure. The fact that Nazi techniques were cruel and the end result evil, whereas Christian techniques are benevolent and the end result beneficial, is beside the point. Both are fundamentally manipulative and therefore do violence to human personality.

One of the most striking features of the ministry of Jesus, as it is portrayed by the gospel writers, is the extreme care he took to leave his friends and acquaintances free to accept or reject the particular insights which he desired to share with them. Whatever the historical facts which lie behind the story of his forty days in the desert at the beginning of his public work, there is in this story a facing by Jesus of the techniques open to him during the time when he was to engage in a preaching and teaching

11

ministry. Each of the temptations led him in the direction of manipulation. Anyone who could solve the economic problems of the age, and thus feed the hungry multitude, could then, as now, be sure of a mass following. Acceptance of the message of love would be a modest price to pay for a full stomach. Similarly the ability to defeat or bring under control the forces of nature was a certain guarantee of powerful influence; how could the claims of a man capable of defying the forces of gravity be resisted? Again, no one could have secured a greater following by the Jewish people of the first century than a man who offered the way to political liberation. Any of these roles would have opened the way to massive acceptance of the particular message which Jesus felt called to share with his fellow men. Yet the message itself demanded that it should be accepted freely and without any trace of coercion. No more than a girl can be compelled to accept the love of a particular boy – how disastrous have been the attempts to apply compulsion in this area of human experience – no more can a man or woman be driven into a position where they have no alternative but to accept the love of God.

Just how clearly Jesus saw this, and how scrupulously he observed its implications in the exercise of his ministry, is to be seen by a careful examination of the gospel records. Attractive stories were used to command attention and to convey meaning, but the response was always left to the individual without any attempt at pressurizing. Here, it may be argued, is the explanation of the apparent ambiguity of much of the teaching of Jesus. Miracles of healing and mysterious involvement in the workings of nature were, not unnaturally, remembered vividly by the gospel writers, yet Jesus did not use his unusual powers in order to attract attention or compel allegiance. On the contrary, those who were healed or who witnessed some supernatural happening were frequently asked to keep the information to themselves. And there is no clearer indication of the freedom which Jesus allowed to his followers than the presence of Judas in the inner circle of the apostolic community. At the very climax of his ministry, at the final supper during the evening before his

12

crucifixion, Jesus was prepared for Judas to exercise his freedom to the extent of desertion and betrayal. His only comment to him was 'What you have to do, do quickly.'

It cannot, however, be concluded from this that Jesus was less than diligent in sharing his insights with others. Even the fragmentary accounts of his life and work provided by the gospels show a man who was totally dedicated to sharing his insights into the nature of reality with as many as could bear to receive them. Without displaying those ominous signs of frenetic activity which characterize the lives of most present-day evangelists, Jesus spared no pains in making himself available to those who would listen to his message or accept his love. In the end this was to cost him his life, but not before he had created the nucleus of a community which, having received his insights, would be committed to sharing them with an ever-widening circle of people.

The emphasis on sharing cannot be over-stressed. The community founded by Jesus was deeply committed to sharing its insights with others, but it was not trained in the art of propaganda, neither were its members commissioned to a ministry of manipulation. They were to treat men and women as human beings who, in their various ways, were struggling to find life's meaning, and in terms of love and friendship offer them the particular insights which they had themselves received through their encounter with Jesus. This called for diligence and much sensitivity, qualities which the apostles possessed in greater and lesser degrees, but it required neither aggression nor threats, and there was no promise of success; only suffering.

While it seems necessary at an early stage in this book to establish as firmly as possible that the communication of the Christian faith is to be seen in terms of sharing and not of manipulative propaganda – a point to which I shall return on a number of occasions later – it would be a serious mistake to suppose that the communication of the Christian faith is *essentially* different from other forms of communication, religious or secular. All are faced with the same kind of problems, all need to use a variety of methods, all are subject to certain (though not always the same) limitations, all encounter barriers of one kind or another, each has its own creative possibilities. Few Christian communicators appear to be aware of the common ground they share with other communicators and of the insights they might receive by acquainting themselves with the work of people who, by study and experience, have discovered ways in which knowledge, insight and experience may be shared. Vague references to the methods apparently used by biblical teachers and writers, with more than a suggestion that these methods form part of the deposit of Christian faith, all too frequently take the place of discussion with journalists, broadcasters, teachers, playwrights, painters and others who are concerned with the communication of information and truth. Yet there is much to be learned from, and shared with, these communicators, as will be seen if the three main types of communication are considered.

1. *The communication of information* Here is common ground shared with the journalist, the teacher and the non-fiction writer, for all of whom 'opinion is free, but facts are sacred'. The Christian communicator can never escape the responsibility of giving as accurate an account as possible of the Christian tradition in its origin and development. This is far from easy, since the Christian faith has a long history and at many crucial points the sources are verbal rather than documentary. Yet the attempt must be made. Any honest enquirer is entitled to a statement of the facts concerning the Christian gospel, facts touching upon background, origins, developments and, of course, articles of belief. This immediately raises the issue of integrity since, in the same way that an honest journalist must be careful to distinguish between the facts as he has observed them and his subsequent interpretation of those facts, so the Christian theologian, apologist and teacher must be as honest as he can about the sources of his information and the points at which fact and interpretation are difficult to disentangle.

Few things have brought the Christian faith into greater disrepute than the unwillingness of its accredited teachers to observe these fundamental rules concerning the communication of information. Opinions have been paraded as facts. Tradition has been confused with events. Dogma has been substituted for reverent agnosticism. The fruits of this are now being reaped in the form of an educated population which believes that the Christian religion is essentially obscurantist and the church a 'zone of untruth', and congregations bewildered by the attempts of younger clergy and ministers to distinguish the heart of the gospel from the various contexts in which it is set. Nowhere is the seriousness of the situation more clearly displayed than at meetings of local pastors who complain bitterly that their work is being undermined by the widely-publicized work of scholars in which attention is called to important historical or dogmatic problems. Without suggesting that scholars are infallible, or that every sermon and article should be an essay in form-criticism, a much greater readiness to admit to uncertainties and to the relationship between the Bible and the continuing Christian tradition seems long overdue. Effective communication requires integrity on the part of the communicator, not least on the part of the Christian communicator who is concerned to present facts concerning one who claimed to be the truth.

2. *The communication of an insight* The common ground here is with philosophers, some politicians and many working in different branches of the arts. The insight may have been received from tradition, obtained through the reasoning of the mind, developed from experience in the fields of individual and social life, or accepted through some form of revelation (however this word be interpreted and explained). In every case, those who believe themselves to possess insight are obliged to eschew the constant temptation to dogmatic utterance. There may have been periods in history when to preface an utterance with the words 'Thus says the Lord' was sufficient to command attention and respect, though the experience of the Hebrew prophets hardly encourages such a view since they were almost universally ignored. But pontificating, whether from ecclesiastical or secular sources (and both are subject to this temptation) is no longer acceptable to modern man and is therefore a highly ineffective method of communication.

Those who believe themselves to possess insight into the working of the human personality or the life of society are required to exercise the patience demanded by dialogue and to be as ready to listen as to speak. As parents know only too well, the transferring of even the most elementary insight to their children is exceedingly difficult. No longer is parental authority sufficient to guarantee credibility. The child has to discover for himself, often 'the hard way', and in that discovery makes a common insight his own. At the political level the transferring of democratic institutions (assuming these to be good things) from western nations to the new countries of Africa and Asia is proving to be virtually impossible. The communication of insight requires the greatest patience and sensitivity, and the willingness of a growing number of Christian theologians to enter into careful dialogue with men of other faiths is an encouraging sign that the nature of truth and the requirements of true communication are being recognized.

A similar sensitivity and patience is called for by the fact that individuals are able to receive insight only when offered to them in particular ways. There are those who receive most clearly when the offering is in visual form. There are those who cope most easily with the verbal. Others assimilate best when the categories employed are spatial or bodily. These differences have to be recognized and taken seriously by all communicators, and the Christian communicator is not exempt from the discipline and flexibility which the variety demands. The comments of the naval gentleman on my sermon at St Martin-in-the-Fields might conceivably have been different had the presentation been in a non-verbal form.

3. *The communication of an experience* This, it need hardly be said, is the most tricky territory of all for the communicator. And the deeper the experience for the individual, or for the community, the more treacherous the ground becomes. Has anyone ever succeeded in conveying to another person what falling in love meant to him? Does the Old Testament account of the Exodus get anywhere near to conveying to its readers what the experience meant, and still means, for the consciousness of the Jewish people? Can the Black American begin to convey to his white compatriots or to people in Europe and Asia what it feels

16

like to belong to a repressed section of a nation which lives beneath a Statue of Liberty? The problems facing those concerned with the communication of religious experience are therefore all too obvious. If I am among those who have profound mystical experiences, how am I able to share this with others who have never had a similar experience? St Paul tried valiantly to convey in words what he experienced while on the road to Damascus, but it may be that we shall get a better insight into his experience by viewing Caravaggio's great painting on the subject, tucked away in a small chapel in the church of Santa Maria del Popolo in Rome. Just how complicated the issue is becomes even more apparent if, while we are in Rome, we visit Bernini's famous sculpture of St Teresa in Ecstasy in the church of Santa Maria dell Vittoria. The only way in which Bernini was able to convey St Teresa's mystical experiences was by providing her with a bodily posture and facial expression which look remarkably close to those characteristic of sexual ecstasy. Now it may be argued that mystical and sexual ecstasy are very closely linked – perhaps even of the same order of human experience – but there are few of today's mystics who would feel able to describe their experience in sexual terms – and even fewer Christians ready to hear and understand them.

It may be that attempts to communicate what has been experienced in life's depths or extremities should be abandoned, and that the advice of Wittgenstein must be accepted: 'Whereof one cannot speak, thereof one must be silent.' Certainly the painter or the musician or the dramatist or the poet seems to be in a better position than the preacher or the writer to convey something of life's deepest meanings. Yet the Christian who has had particular experiences of God's love and power and peace often feels under a compelling obligation to share his experience with others. In these circumstances he must not be surprised if he fails to communicate or is completely misunderstood. The most cogent expression of his experience will be conveyed through the effect which it has had upon his own visible being. The supreme example here is provided by Jesus himself, who was in many ways a highly unsuccessful verbal communicator but whose life and death have communicated meaning across the centuries and through the barriers which make communication between men difficult, if not actually impossible.

This brings us to a consideration of some of the barriers to human communication which, once again, place the Christian communicator and all other communicators on common ground and which have to be taken seriously by those who wish to share their Christian knowledge, insight and experience with their fellow human beings. The subject is, not surprisingly, a highly complex one which continues to exercise the minds of students of psychology, language, philosophy and sociology. There is no consensus of view to be discovered among them, but a fairly simple illustration may help to pinpoint the chief barriers to communication at every level and provide food for thought, if not for action, for those who wonder why the Christian 'good news' so frequently fails to reach those to whom it is directed.

I may wish to communicate by radio an important piece of information to someone in Australia whom I once met briefly, but whom I don't know at all well. My message is transmitted, but I fail to get a response. What is the explanation? There are several possibilities. Perhaps the Australian's receiving set was not equipped to pick up my message. It may be that the transmission was subject to so much external interference, or that the location of his receiver was so noisy, that he failed to hear properly what I was saying. It may be that the necessarily brief nature of my message was misinterpreted by him because of certain assumptions, partly-conscious or unconscious, on his part. It may be that I presented my message badly and conveyed only confusion; perhaps I took too much for granted. Or it may even have been that neither my transmitter nor his receiver were working properly and that there was therefore no effective channel of communication between us.

Translate this illustration into the work of the Christian communicator and the causes of 'failure' may become somewhat clearer. Not everyone is able to hear what we are saying; this may be a temporary phase of their life or it may be that, for a variety of reasons, the Christian faith is not their way to happiness and fulfilment. Others fail to pick up what we are saying because they are distracted by what are for them, at that particular moment, more important messages. Another common cause of breakdown in Christian communication is provided by divergence or incompatibility of assumptions; an increasing problem in a world where there is no single view of the nature of the universe and of ultimate reality. The chances that our presentation of the gospel is confused and confusing are always real, and we all too readily assume that we have established a most effective channel of communication with either an individual or a group when, in fact, the line is quite dead. It would be stretching the interpretation of the parable of the sower much too far to point to a confirmation of this analysis, but the parable does at least indicate that Jesus was well aware that in its efforts to communicate his gospel of love the apostolic community would be faced with a *variety* of barriers.

# 2  What is There to Communicate?

Much, if not all, of the first chapter has taken for granted a particular view or interpretation of the Christian gospel. And what is to follow in the remainder of this book will also be based on the same interpretation. It would therefore be an aid to clarity if this interpretation were to be stated in a reasonably brief compass, and at the same time the crucial question were raised of what, if anything, Christians are trying to communicate. The most efficient channel of communication is of little value if there is nothing worth transmitting through it.

What follows is necessarily a personal statement. It owes a great deal to tradition past and present, and makes no claim to originality or infallibility. If any readers find it unhelpful, I shall be sorry but hope that they may be wise enough to move on to the next chapter without having spent too much time on this one. If any readers are in possession of what seems to them a better understanding of the Christian faith, they will have cause for gratitude. By the time these words appear in print I may wish to offer a few amendments myself, but I can only offer a statement which approximates as closely as possible to my own under- standing of the truth and to my own experience. Whether it complies with the canons of orthodoxy I do not know, nor am I greatly concerned.

I begin, as indeed I shall end, with a man named Jesus who lived and died just over nineteen centuries ago. For my know- ledge of this man I am primarily indebted to the tradition of the community which he founded, and through which certain facts concerning his life and teaching have been transmitted across the ages. The Bible, and in particular the New Testament, forms a crucial part of that tradition, and provides a deposit of faith and doctrine against which subsequent developments may be checked. But I am not entirely dependent on the testimony of others for my acquaintance with Jesus. Every Sunday, and more frequently if I so choose, I join with a group of those who form the contemporary embodiment of the community of Jesus and we share in a meal which includes elements of memorial, fellowship and hope. The origin of this meal may be traced to the supper which Jesus arranged for his closest friends on the night before his crucifixion and at which he promised his continuing presence with them, a presence of which they would be specially conscious whenever they met together for a similar meal. When I share in that meal – the Eucharist, the Mass, the Holy Communion, the Lord's Supper – I am aware of that promise being fulfilled. In the re-enactment of that occasion of memory, fellowship and hope I find myself brought into the presence not only of a mixed bunch of my fellow human beings, but also into the presence of one whose life is united with the depths of my own being. A similar experience is available to me in my all too rare moments of quiet reflection and recollection, in my reading of the Bible and (sometimes) when I am confronted with deep human suffering.

Psychiatrists and others may seek to explain my experience and that of other Christians in terms of unfulfilled human needs of one kind or another. And there are occasions when I would warmly welcome such an explanation and 'release', for the experience of the presence of Jesus is not always convenient or comforting. But this is not my situation at the moment, and I cannot escape from encounters with Jesus, neither can I refuse to acknowledge the claims which he makes upon me without undermining my own struggle for integrity and integration. So I am 'landed' with Jesus, as a person who belongs to history, who has shaped the course of history in a remarkable fashion, and who is constantly impinging upon my own life and experience. I am also aware of the fact that a large number of my fellow human beings are similarly 'landed' with the Man of Nazareth.

Returning to the Jesus tradition and to those elements in it which find written expression in the New Testament, I am made vividly aware of the fact that central to the life and teaching of

Jesus is the concept of the kingdom of God. Jesus employed various forms of teaching and performed various actions – some quite straightforward, others most mysterious – yet all were inextricably connected with his fundamental belief concerning the kingdom of God. What does this involve? I am able to identify eight specific and inter-related elements in the gospel of the kingdom.

1. This is God's world. Here is a piece of shorthand which, in the world of the twentieth century, undoubtedly requires a good deal of translation before it can become meaningful to a large number of people. The form of the translation may vary a good deal, but in the end it must convey an understanding that the universe is neither accidental nor arbitrary, but at the heart of all life there is a power which is supernatural, yet personal. No proof of this can be offered, or should be attempted, in terms and categories employed by scientists, but the thesis is capable of surviving close philosophical scrutiny and forms part of the dynamic experience of the Christian believer.

2. God is present and active in his world. Again, the shorthand requires translation for the twentieth-century reader; this time the emphasis is placed upon the fact that the creative, personal power whom Christians call God, and which is known by other names in other religions, is neither remote nor passive, but is at the very centre of life and involved in the continuity of its existence through the process of creation. This is not to say that God is to be identified exclusively with the universe, since the creator inevitably transcends his creation. It is to say that those who wish to become aware of God's presence and activity must seek it within this world, and especially in those parts of the world in which they are themselves most deeply involved.

3. God has a plan and purpose for the world. This immediately brings us into the vast arena of debate concerning developments in the natural order, the nature of causality, the possibility of real human freedom, the workings of providence and, at a less sophisticated level, the bewilderment felt by most people when faced with actual suffering. These are not subjects for discussion in a few brief paragraphs, and when all the books have been

22

written and the debates concluded, the Christian can not do more – or less – than assert that his act of faith, buttressed by experience, does not conflict with his intellectual integrity. Much Christian apologetic in this area of religious belief and experience has been less than adequate, but it is quite crucial for the Christian position that while the workings of God are certainly mysterious they are in no sense arbitrary or purposeless, neither do they run counter to his nature which is love.

4. God's plan for the world moves nearer to its realization whenever human beings accept one another in love. Since God is himself the complete embodiment of love and is at work in the world as the 'cosmic lover', his presence and purpose is discerned most clearly whenever and wherever love breaks out in human experience. For the purpose of brevity the chief sign of this love in action may be described in terms of acceptance. It is when men and women accept one another, unconditionally, and without possessiveness or an eye to manipulation and exploitation, that love is experienced at its deepest level. This opens the way for the lives of individuals and communities to discover liberation, justice, service, hope and joy – all of which are known, by experience, to be life-enhancing and therefore pearls beyond price. It is in God's loving purpose that man should possess these pearls.

5. God's plan and purpose is, however, frequently thwarted by the presence in this world of forces or influences which run counter to the creative power of love. There is little of value to be gained by speculation concerning the origin of these forces or the way in which they are perpetuated. Some Christians have found it helpful to focus them in the person of a devil. Many learned volumes have been written on the fall and original sin. Significantly, the Bible indulges in little speculation on the subject; its writers evidently preferring to concentrate on the fact that destructive forces are actually at work in individuals and in human society and that the main task is to get rid of them or, at least, reduce their power to cause suffering. Here it is necessary for the twentieth-century Christian to recognize that a great deal of what was once attributed to mysterious evil forces, personal or impersonal, has been eliminated by the discoveries and prescriptions

of modern science. This is clearly a matter for rejoicing since the Christian faith is concerned with the overcoming of all that defaces man's humanity and only engages in metaphysical discussion in so far as this assists towards that end. It is not beyond the bounds of possibility that psychology may produce an explanation of and an antidote for what Christians now call sin. It may be that a coalition of sociologists and politicians will discover the source of destructiveness in human society and offer a complete cure for man's social ills. But even the most optimistic members of these professions will not deny that such explanations and prescriptions lie some way into the future. And among the more open and discerning of their number is a growing recognition that the more effectively certain social and personal diseases are cured, the more starkly exposed are other problems which are less easily accessible to the tools of science and seem to be embedded in, or intertwined with, the very heart of man and society. The battle against them must continue with all possible skill and speed, but the supernatural element has not yet been demonstrated as irrelevant or redundant.

6. In the life and ministry of Jesus we are not only told of the existence of the kingdom of God, shown signs of its life, and provided with hints as to how its power of love may be existentially experienced, we are also shown how many of the forces opposed to God's purpose and plan may be overcome. Christians ascribe divinity to Jesus, not because they believe his birth and life to represent the invasion of the world by a divine being from some other sphere, but because they see in him the perfect embodiment of that love which they believe lies at the heart of the universe and belongs to the being of God himself. In Jesus the love which is the creative power of the universe, and occupies a place at the centre of every human life, was perfectly expressed. This is not to suggest that Jesus was exempt from normal human limitations. On the contrary, it is to emphasize that God's love was revealed in and through a life which was at every point like our own. No other revelation or manifestation of love would have been remotely helpful to us in our struggle to realize our humanity to the full. A Jesus who was in some way specially privileged

could not have appeared as the example of what man is, and is capable of becoming. Those who emphasize the uniqueness of Jesus at the expense of his essential humanity do a signal disservice to the truth and make man's quest for a life in which love is more perfectly expressed infinitely more difficult. In fact, far from appearing in a privileged role, Jesus is more easily identified with the underprivileged. The picture of Jesus portrayed by the gospels and carried through the mainstream Christian tradition is one of a man who lacked what most western people regard as the necessities of life, who had little in the way of support at either the personal or social levels and had more than the normal share of physical and mental suffering. But it is precisely because love was expressed to perfection through such an underprivileged man that we have the hope and possibility of its fuller expression in our own lives. Much of the suffering endured by Jesus is attributable to the inevitable conflict between the divine love and the forces of anti-love which was focused in his life and which in the end led to his death. He always met destructive evil with the simplicity of creative love, and this was the heart of his life and teaching. There is nothing romantic or sentimental about this. There is no guarantee that those who face evil with love will escape suffering. Quite the contrary. But there is in the life of Jesus the most vivid illustration of the truth that those who face evil with love are liberated from bondage to evil and freed to exercise that creativity – in relationships and interior growth – which belongs to man's essential humanity. Love opens the door to freedom, and the story of the resurrection – however this be explained in physical terms – is the climax of this fundamental insight or revelation.

7. It is open to every man and woman to find the way to freedom by accepting the presence of love at the centre of their being and, through identification with Jesus, who lived as a historical person and is still to be encountered in faith, begin to remove the obstacles which prevent the fullest expression of that love in an individual's daily life. The Christian gospel is not concerned with the transformation of the human into the superhuman; rather is its task to transform the inhuman into the truly

human. Within every human being there is a vast potentiality for good. The human body is itself a miracle of integrated ingenuity. The capacity of the human mind seems almost limitless and continues to expand at a pace which would be breathtaking were it not now taken for granted. The depth of relationship which can develop between individuals, inside and outside marriage, is perhaps life's most creative mystery. When the biblical writers speak of man as the crown of creation, they mean precisely what they say. Amidst the many wonders and beauties of the universe, none is more glorious than a human life whose potentialities are being fully realized. Later theologians have sometimes overlooked or distorted this truth in order to emphasize that which distinguishes man from his creator, but St Irenaeus had deeper insight when he wrote 'The glory of God is a man fully alive.' The Christian gospel is therefore offered to man to enable him to become what he potentially is, a mature human being in whose life love is the dominating force. Jesus stands before the human race as such a man. He is a manifestation of what man truly is, and what we are all capable of becoming once we allow love to take control of our lives. This is the meaning of salvation, which is the only and final end of the Christian religion.

8. Although the kingdom of God is already in existence and its power and purpose seen in special focus in the life and ministry of Jesus, it will not be fully accepted and fulfilled in the time scale of human history but must await the end of time when all things are, in some as yet inconceivable way, caught up into the loving purposes of their creator. The Christian faith is the most this-worldly, materialistic religion of all the great world religions. The concept of the kingdom of God is concerned with this present world: 'Thy kingdom come. Thy will be done on earth as it is in heaven.' God is the creator of this world; it is his. His life and love are interwoven into every part of the created order. The gospel is concerned with man, as he is and where he is. Salvation is offered to every man and the whole of mankind in and through every facet of life. There is no part of man's life and being which lies outside the realm of that love which leads to freedom and fulfilment. God revealed his love most fully in the life of a human

26

being who expressed that love in the rough and tumble of life on this earth. All attempts to present the Christian faith as if its primary concern was with what happens to a man after his death, a common feature of much manipulative evangelism, are nothing more than a total distortion and denial of the Christianity of the New Testament and of the mainstream Christian tradition. They must be resisted and, where possible, corrected. Having said this, however, it is necessary to add that because the Christian faith is so materialistic in its concerns, it is also realistic in its expectations. Although the immense potentiality of man is recognized and rejoiced in, and although the Christian has seen in Jesus what man truly is and is capable of becoming, experience and insight combine to make it plain that the forces of destruction are firmly entrenched in human life at every level. Love is capable of loosing man from all that enslaves him, yet many of the marks of slavery remain with him through his life and the scars of injury and grief cannot be ignored. This is true at the personal level, and even more true at the social level. There is a proper form of Christian utopianism which looks forward to the day when human society is ordered in such a way that men and women can live in an environment where the sources of much of today's suffering have been removed. The possibilities here are boundless, and the Christian who has caught the vision of the kingdom of God cannot cease from striving to create a more just and happier society. Yet involvement in this struggle immediately brings individuals and groups face to face with the power and reality of human weakness and selfishness. The fruits of massive political effort are often meagre. Change brought about through spectacular revolution, violent or not, is frequently disappointing in its consequences. Pioneers of change rarely reap the longed-for harvest, and must be content with the realization, or merely the hope, that they have made some little contribution to the welfare of those who will come after them. In these circumstances, which it must be emphasized are the normal conditions of human activity, the temptation to cynicism and despair is often overwhelming. It is the special gift and joy of youth to be possessed of high ideals, yet how few of these are sustained into and through the middle years of life. Political leaders of all kinds nearly always begin their careers with the intention of serving their fellow men regardless of the cost to themselves, yet how quickly the lust for power and the thirst of ambition takes over from the original altruism. How then is the dynamic of creative change to be maintained? Some men and women are sustained throughout a lifetime of disappointment by an unbridled optimism. They believe that something better always lies just round the corner and thus they avoid the pains of despair. But the number of those who can live in this way is relatively small and it is far from obvious that resorting to optimism to escape from reality is either creative or healthy. Christian hope is grounded in realism concerning the present and a faith in the future which is not escapist but provides the dynamic for immediate action in the here and now. Jesus taught his followers that they would not experience God's love in all its fulness in this life, and that the new heaven and new earth which were to be the corporate expression of and fulfilment of that love would not be established in their time. Yet the promise of the ultimate fulfilment of God's loving purpose was firm and the demand was made that the Christian believer should, like Jesus himself, anticipate the future by living in the power of love in the present. Through the death of Jesus on the cross the way to love's ultimate victory is now open. Those who travel along that way can anticipate what lies ahead and, as they journey, express their hope in concrete acts of love.

The kingdom of God, which the Christian wishes to share with others, involves the individual and the community of faith in a process of looking back to the life and ministry of Jesus, in a deep commitment to the present where the kingdom is to be more clearly recognized and established, and in a longing for the future when all the obstacles to the kingdom have been removed and the beauty and perfection of God's love is experienced in all its glory.

This is the knowledge, the insight and the experience which the Christian longs to share with others. Its compelling power has over the centuries provided the imperative of Christian mission. Its mystery must produce in the man of faith a deepening sense of wonder and humility.

# 3  Across the Centuries

On occasions when they have nothing more pressing to occupy their attention, theologians sometimes turn to consider why Jesus never wrote a book, or indeed why he seems to have written nothing at all apart from the ephemeral piece of writing on the ground mentioned in some versions of St John's account of his discussion with the Pharisees about the woman taken in adultery. There can of course be no answer to this question and, though arguments from silence are notoriously hazardous, the fact that Jesus did not commit his insights to paper might at least encourage a little more caution amongst those who roundly declare Christianity to be the religion of a book or who believe that the world will become more Christian in direct proportion to the number of Bibles and religious tracts distributed.

The tools of communication inherited by the apostolic community are clearly described in Acts 2.24, where we are told that those who became Christians on the day of Pentecost were baptized and then devoted themselves to the apostles' teaching and fellowship, to the breaking of bread and the prayers. Here it is possible to distinguish three separate, though obviously interrelated, means of communication: the verbal sharing of the gospel as it had been revealed by Jesus to the apostles, the symbolism involved in the actions of baptism and breaking of bread, and the fellowship experienced within the life of the community of faith.

On the evidence available to us, these were the only means of communication employed by the church for the first quarter of a century of its life. Given the eschatological expectations of the early church, it is perhaps not surprising that no attempt was made to move into less spontaneous fields of communication.

29

But, even though his letters were sometimes more powerful than his presence, St Paul appears to have been a reluctant writer, and the fact that the gospels are relatively late suggests that no one was particularly anxious to commit the gospel to writing until it became absolutely imperative that they should do so. Certainly, the absence of written texts did not inhibit the church's missionary activity, and though it is no purpose of this book to discourage the wider and more skilful use of modern means of communication, one is bound to notice that at certain periods of its life the church has managed rather well on limited communications resources and thus one is bound to stress that the harnessing of sophisticated communications techniques is not in itself any guarantee that the gospel will be effectively communicated.

Thanks to the work of C. H. Dodd and others, it is possible to discover with a fair degree of accuracy the basic content of the apostolic preaching, with its heavy emphasis on the significance of the death and resurrection of Jesus and his promised return. The recognition that the gospels consist mainly of the early church's teaching material also gives a fairly clear idea of what the church was concerned to share with others. Even when due allowance is made for the developed memories of a non-literary people, it is obvious that the words of Jesus himself had made a marked impression on the minds of those who were his close companions. Christian communicators in every age are therefore bound to take account of the techniques which Jesus employed.

New Testament scholars appear to be more or less agreed that we are nearest to the actual words of Jesus when we read the parables. The reasons for this opinion need not detain us here, but no one is surprised to learn that stories are the most easily remembered form of verbal communication. Furthermore, mankind has discovered by experience that the deepest truths about life can normally be shared only by means of stories. Bald statements or carefully reasoned arguments are not only less memorable, they are also less meaningful than the carefully compiled and narrated story. Here, however, it is important to note that the parables of the kingdom told by Jesus were not simply contrived stories to illustrate some abstract truth. They were stories about situations which the listeners might easily encounter during the course of their daily lives, and so they were taught that the kingdom of God was directly concerned with life in the fields, in the home, in the market place and in normal human relationships.

Jesus also made use of arresting sayings, which aroused the attention of his listeners and prepared the way for the sharing of further insight. On the evidence of the gospels, it was the saying, rather than anything which followed, that left the most lasting impression, since many of the sayings of Jesus now stand in isolation. But if the parables provide a guide to the teaching technique of Jesus, it may be that his striking sayings were not always followed by detailed exposition. Jesus does not appear to have been particularly concerned to spell out the precise significance of everything he said and did, preferring to leave certain words and actions with his audience and allowing them the opportunity to work out the meaning for themselves, within the context of their own experience.

Integrated with the parables and the sayings was a life which, in itself, was a communication of the truth concerning the kingdom of God. In his love of individuals, the child, the paralysed man, the prostitute, the criminal and those who engineered his death, he disclosed the meaning and implications of life in the kingdom. And the supreme disclosure came through his crucifixion, hence the emphasis on this aspect of his work in the subsequent preaching of men whose hearts and minds had been deeply touched by the event. Through the acceptance in love of undeserved suffering lay the route to resurrection. So the life of Jesus still communicates meaning to many who have little knowledge of his actual teaching.

This, then, was the content of the gospel and the method of sharing it with others bequeathed to the apostolic community. And in the remainder of the New Testament we are given glimpses of how a few of the members of that community tried to carry it into effect. The preaching of St Paul evidently met with a varied reception and it is important to notice the variety of methods attributed to him by the author of the Acts of the Apostles.

Sometimes he took the opportunity to address synagogue congregations, using the Jewish scriptures as his starting point. On at least one occasion, in Athens, he moved from the pagan beliefs of an outdoor audience to a declaration of his own convictions about the God whose nature was revealed in Jesus Christ. There were times when he hired a hall and held discussions with any who were prepared to engage in conversation with him. Frequently he shared his beliefs with individuals and sometimes he spoke to groups of people meeting in houses. Then, as the church became established in various parts of the Mediterranean world, Paul found it necessary to write letters to particular churches, sometimes to groups of churches in a certain geographical area. In these letters he nearly always stressed that they were a substitute for a personal visit and regretted that it was impossible at the time to convey his message verbally.

Preaching and conversation were, however, only one aspect of the infant church's communicating role. In the administration of baptism, individuals and the church community entered into a dramatic and sacramental experience of the death and resurrection of Christ. Through the immersion of a convert in water, it was demonstrated that the kingdom of God involved the believer in a new, liberated life where enslavement to sin belonged to the past. The symbolism of washing and rising were powerful means of communicating or confirming an experienced truth. Similarly with the breaking of the bread. On the first day of the week the Christian community in every place gathered for a meal at which they declared the fact of Christ's risen presence in their midst by re-enacting the supper which he had held with his closest friends during the night before his death. The survival of this action down the centuries as the central point in the Christian community's life is ample testimony to its communicating power. John Wesley spoke of the Eucharist as 'a converting ordinance' and it is at the Christian altar that millions of people have been given a vision of life in the kingdom of God which no verbal description could ever match.

Along with the spoken word and the liturgical action went the quality of life experienced within and exhibited by the local churches. Although the sharing of material possessions did not survive the rapid expansion of the church, it symbolized in the earliest days the intensity of fellowship which existed among the Christian believers. That this fellowship was not always expressed to perfection is abundantly clear from reading the Acts of the Apostles and the Epistles, but the importance attached to the healing of divisions and the care of those in need is an indication of the quality of life expected of the Christian community. In a harsh world, where life was cheap and individuals counted for little in the eyes of the state, the existence of groups of people trying to live out the love which lies at the heart of the kingdom of God was a most powerful expression of the gospel. This affected those who experienced it at first hand and did not go unnoticed by others who were out of sympathy with the church but were aware of the motivation of its life. The careful training by Jesus of the original apostolic community had not been in vain.

Space forbids a detailed discussion of how the church moved into the area of written communication which led eventually to the formation of the canon of the New Testament. In any case, the subject is more than adequately dealt with elsewhere. But certain aspects of this development require brief comment here. The great variety of approach shown by the early Christian writers is significant. The gospels are supreme examples of this. Although each is concerned with recording the main facts concerning the life and teaching of Jesus, the approach of the four writers is quite different. The personal factor was doubtless important – certain events and teachings making a deep impression on a particular writer – but of even greater importance was the fact that the writer was attempting to communicate with, or on behalf of, a particular group of people. Hence the different treatment of the subject. The needs and outlook of the readers could not be ignored. Similarly with the epistles which were addressed to particular individuals and communities and, naturally, reflect the situations and concerns of their recipients. The contrast between the New Testament and a twentieth-century work of systematic theology is complete.

The rich variety of material in the New Testament is also

closely related to its spontaneity. The writers were not learned men with ample time for theological reflection. They were heavily engaged in missionary activity and only put pen to paper when driven to do so in order to meet certain specific needs. These needs dictated the content of the documents and their form. They were spontaneous and situational. We must also remember that the number of people who actually read any of the original New Testament documents, or the copies which were circulated later, must have been relatively small. They were not available in cheap paperback editions for the bookstalls of the primitive house churches, and in any case the level of literacy in the early Christian communities was extremely low. Which is not to deny that the New Testament writings were influential. Manifestly they were. But their influence is to be traced to the use made of them by the leaders of the churches who read them to the congregations and incorporated them into their own preaching.

Similar points must be made about much of the writing which emerged during the four centuries that followed. Although there came into existence schools of reflective theologians, who were concerned to investigate and articulate the intellectual aspects of the teaching of Jesus, it is still possible to discern great variety in their work. Most of them were trying to relate their faith to particular philosophical systems current at the time or to correct what appeared to be distortions or misrepresentations of the original gospel. St Augustine was driven to write his greatest theological work by the unmistakable signs of break-up in the social and political order of his day. Here again, one is bound to take note of the fact that the readership of the most formative works of Christian theology was extremely small. Illiteracy and the most obvious difficulties in the reproduction of manuscripts made this inevitable.

So it continued to be until the revolution brought about by Johann Gutenberg's invention of printing by moveable type in 1454. During the tenth century in England the Benedictine Abbot Aelfric produced vernacular translations of the Bible and the early Christian fathers, together with two series of homilies which covered the church's year and were designed to help

34

country priests to introduce their people to the thought of St Augustine. But these were unable to leap the communications gap created by illiteracy and reproduction problems. The same was, perhaps fortunately, true of the Blickling Homilies which aimed to prepare people for the anticipated end of the world in the year 1000. Throughout the Middle Ages Bible reading was extremely rare and, although manuscript books played an extremely influential part in the development of Christian theology and worship, the fact remains that the written word has not been very significant in the *direct* communication of the Christian faith until the present century. The church did of course make considerable use of the new opportunities offered by printing, and the use by the printing and publishing industries today of phrases such as 'Father of the Chapel' and 'justification of type' is a pointer to the intimate relationship which existed between churchmen and the early printers, but while illiteracy was the normal condition of the overwhelming majority of ordinary people there was little scope for communication by the written word.

We must therefore now examine some of the alternative means of communication employed by the church during the past nineteen centuries.

*Preaching*

The sharing of Christian insight and experience by means of the spoken word has been recognized as a primary means of communication for the whole of the church's history, though there have been periods, sometimes of considerable duration, when preaching has been seriously neglected or quite inadequate in its content. The importance of preaching was stressed by many of the early Christian fathers, especially by St Ambrose, St Augustine, Pope Leo and Gregory the Great, who made a particular point of emphasizing the need for preachers to make ample use of illustrations. Augustine, doubtless influenced by his own early training in the art of rhetoric, said that 'eloquence is a handmaid of truth', though subsequent history was soon to show that it could serve error with equal facility. In Britain, the Celtic missionaries were, according to Bede, great preachers and the Council of Clovesho (747) not only enjoined bishops and priests to be diligent in the exercising of their preaching office, but also gave directions concerning the content of sermons. By the eve of the Norman Conquest preaching was established as a normal part of the church's work. Canons issued in England in 960, as a result of the work of St Dunstan, required the clergy to preach every Sunday, and the Capitula of Theodulf (994) said that every priest should have 'a school of learners' in his house and teach them free of charge.

That those who professed to be followers of Jesus the teacher laid considerable emphasis on preaching is hardly surprising, yet we find that by the thirteenth century sermons were rare and teaching outside the monastic schools barely recognizable as a form of Christian communication. The reason for this decline is not easy to discover, though some historians have suggested that an increased emphasis on the confessional and the sacrament of penance during this period may have led to the belief that public preaching and teaching was unnecessary.

Not until the emergence of the mendicant orders in the thirteenth century did preaching come into its own again. Both the Dominicans and the Franciscans regarded preaching as their primary function and brought to the task of Christian communication a new zeal and a new approach. The Dominicans, deeply aware of the need to harness Christian conviction to the philosophical presuppositions of their day, brought Aristotle and Christ together in what we may now consider to be an uneasy, if not actually incompatible, union, but which dominated European thought for the next five centuries. Their effective preaching of the Crusades offers a neat commentary on the dangers, as well as the benefits, of eloquence. The Franciscans were of course particularly concerned to communicate the gospel to 'God's poor' and believed the sermon to be a crucial instrument in this task. One of their greatest preachers, St Bernardino of Siena (1380–1444) wrote: 'If of these two things you can do only one – either hear the Mass or hear the sermon – you should let the Mass go, rather than the sermon. . . . There is less peril for your soul in not hearing Mass, than in not hearing the sermon.' Many of the friars echoed this belief and one can only suppose that the style and content of the mendicant sermon was more edifying than that of a large proportion of those who later entered the pulpits which they caused to be placed in the cathedrals and parish churches of Europe.

The Lollards shared many of the gifts and ideals of the friars, particularly during the second phase of their work in the early part of the fifteenth century, and were especially concerned to correct what they believed to be the errors which had crept into popular Franciscan and Dominican preaching. They based their sermons rigorously on the Bible but fell into the trap which awaits every Christian communicator: they failed to take account of the outlook and needs of their listeners. Hence their lack of real success.

The Reformers of the sixteenth and seventeenth centuries laid tremendous emphasis on preaching and shook Christendom with the force and content of their message. But the influence of the Reformers on the preaching in local churches was less significant than might appear from the upheaval caused by the Reformation. The abuses in the mediaeval church against which they inveighed, particularly the ignorance and corruption of the parish clergy, did not provide an adequate base from which an effective revival in preaching could be inaugurated. The friars had exercised a peripatetic preaching ministry of considerable importance but they had been substitutes for the local, resident priest and their work did little to improve the general level of preaching. Without such an improvement it was impossible to secure a permanent growth in Christian communication and the fact that the Church of England found it necessary to publish Books of Homilies in 1547 and 1571 is a clear indication of the current lack of confidence in the ability of the clergy to preach and in their acceptance of Reformation doctrines.

When a point has been reached at which it is necessary to provide preachers with ready-made sermons, it hardly seems too much of an exaggeration to speak of the disappearance of preaching in England. During the seventeenth century John Donne,

George Herbert, Jeremy Taylor and Lancelot Andrewes kept the torch of preaching alight, and towards the end of the century John Tillotson offered a way of preaching 'prudential morality' which was to become the model for many eighteenth-century preachers. But it was not until John Wesley and the evangelical revival that preaching again became influential in Britain. That the people were ready for such a revival is demonstrated by the response which Wesley and his followers evoked. Preaching in the open air, after Anglican pulpits were closed to him, Wesley frequently addressed crowds of 20,000 or more. His journal records one of the most remarkable episodes in Christian history during which a man travelled an average of 8,000 miles a year on horseback and preached thousands of sermons at every conceivable, and inconceivable, hour of day and night. The effect was not only to change the course of church history in Britain, but also the course of the nation's social history. The existence in the declining Methodism of today of some eighteen thousand local preachers testifies to the importance which Wesley's followers have always attached to preaching, though it must not be supposed that Wesley regarded preaching as the only means of communication. His use of music and the formation of groups exhibiting the marks of holiness were equally important in the growth of the Methodist movement.

Charles Simeon and other evangelical leaders helped to make the nineteenth century the greatest preaching and missionary era since the earliest days of the church. The rapid growth of impersonal industrial communities in Britain provided a background against which mass assemblies could easily flourish, and the presence in a town of a gifted orator was sufficient to guarantee a large and attentive audience. This in turn provided a stimulus for the preacher and so the nineteenth century saw in every part of the church a succession of men who took the responsibility of preaching with the greatest seriousness. Their sermons now read strangely to the twentieth-century mind, but they provided an influential segment of Victorian society with substantial material for reflection, and action at both personal and social levels. It was, however, only a segment of society. Large though the congregations undoubtedly were in city churches manned by a gifted preacher, the overwhelming majority of Englishmen never heard a sermon, for the simple reason that they rarely resorted to the places where sermons were to be heard. Recognition of the undoubted greatness of many Victorian preachers must be accompanied by acknowledgment that in their time the churches failed to communicate the gospel to the English people as a whole.

The reasons for this failure cannot be analysed here, but a widespread acceptance of the fact that preaching was largely ineffective as an instrument of mission, added to an even wider mistrust of oratorical propaganda, has caused considerable scepticism about the value of preaching in the twentieth century. Not surprisingly, the general standard of contemporary preaching is low and a growing number of young clergymen believe that the sermon has no valid place in Christian worship, nor indeed in any part of the church's life. In these circumstances, it will be surprising if attempts to train ordination candidates in the art of preaching, and to refresh their elder brethren by means of College of Preachers courses, do much to change the situation during the remaining years of this century.

## Visual arts

The use of visual symbols goes back to the earliest days of the church. The fish was used as a symbol of Christ, of baptism and also of the Eucharist in the early centuries of Christianity and examples of its use, along with the dove and bread, are still to be seen in the catacombs. Freed from the Jewish fear that emblems and pictures would encourage idolatry, the early Christians were also ready to decorate the walls of the catacombs with pictures of events which had significance for faith. Paintings of Noah's ark, the sacrifice of Isaac, Jonah, Daniel in the lions' den, the adoration of the magi, the Good Shepherd and the raising of Lazarus, besides representations of the crucifixion, have been discovered in the catacombs of Rome and are amongst the most moving reminders of the character of primitive Christianity. Of particular interest is the fact that the early church was not afraid to make use of pagan symbolism, interpreting it so that it might serve as a form of Christian communication.

There is no better place to see the early use and development of Christian art than the lovely church of Santa Costanza, in Rome. Built in the early part of the fourth century to house the tomb of Princess Constantia, who had erected the nearby Basilica of Santa Agnese, the mosaics on the vaulting are classical in their symbolism. Set against a white background, reminiscent of the ancient Roman mosaics, the designs are sometimes geometrical, sometimes floral. Sprays of flowers and fruit, vine tendrils, birds, cupid-like figures and other secular symbols predominate, and there are portrayals of the vintage among a number of traditiona lsecular scenes. As far as one can see, there is no particular Christian symbolism here and no one has yet discovered how these graceful and delicately coloured mosaics were interpreted by those who first worshipped in the building. They may well have been content with their intrinsic beauty and representation of the glory of the natural order. The sarcophagus of the princess does, however, provide an example of the way in which classical pagan symbols were adapted to serve Christian insights. The reliefs include sheep, together with peacocks, whose flesh was once believed to be incorruptible, and there are, again, vintage scenes which evoke the imagery of the True Vine. Further development is to be seen in a number of later (probably fifth century) mosaics which portray Jesus giving the keys to Peter and peace to the world. Garlands of foliage and fruit are still used to provide these scenes with borders. Unfortunately, the original mosaics in the dome were destroyed during the sixteenth century and replaced by the present frescoes, but an artist of the time made copies of them in his sketch-book and these indicate that the scenes were of a completely secular character, though some iconographers have suggested that they represented an early attempt to portray the river Jordan, a subject common in later mosaics.

From these early beginnings, Christian art developed quickly and widely. Naturally, mosaics have been most easily preserved from primitive times, but there was ample use of wall paintings and Gregory the Great, writing at the end of the sixth century, said: 'Painting can do for the illiterate what writing does for those who can read.' From the fifth century onwards, the church in the East began to make use of icons, which were an attempt to portray the heavenly kingdom in visual terms. But these were, and are, more than visual aids. Eastern Christians believe that the saints exercise power through them. By the eighth century, however, icons, and visual art generally, had become a subject of controversy in the Eastern Church and all religious art was forbidden. Ostensibly this was because the Emperor, Leo III, thought they were an obstacle to the conversion of Jews and Moslems, but many other political and theological factors were involved and by the tenth century the ban on pictures and icons had been lifted. Interestingly, though the early church was quite ready to use wall paintings and mosaics, sometimes with pagan and secular symbols, it was firmly against the use of statues. It seems that the pagan use of statues was so extensive and so offensive to the Christian mind that their use as an adjunct of Christian worship and a means of communication was considered too dangerous. The Celtic missionaries in Britain, however, showed no reluctance to erect stone crosses and there were wall paintings in many of the Saxon churches.

By the twelfth century sculptors were free to decorate the Romanesque churches which were being erected all over Europe and the next four centuries were to see the Christian faith providing the inspiration for one of the most creative eras in the history of art. Whether the church would have been such a generous patron of the arts had other means of communication been available is an open question. Certainly its concern did not long outlive the invention of printing and it may not be altogether coincidental that those parts of the church which have laid the greatest emphasis on the spoken word have produced the ugliest buildings. But the ordinary Christian who entered a church in the fourteenth century found himself transported into a world of visual imagery so rich as to be almost overwhelming. The pointed arches and soaring roof 'made infinity visible'.

Exquisitely carved statues reminded him of the glory and the goodness of the patriarchs, prophets and saints who had trodden the Christian way before him. Frescoes and other wall paintings in vivid colours portrayed stories from the Bible and from the lives of the saints. Stained glass, by then well developed as an art form, glowed in the windows and provided further instalments from 'the poor man's Bible'. Over the chancel arch was a graphic portrayal of the Last Judgment, indicating what agonies of body, mind and spirit awaited those who were consigned to hell. No detail was spared from these doom paintings and one wonders what the effect of them was on the minds and lives of the unsophisticated people who spent many hours in their presence. But the way to avoid the pains of hell was portrayed equally dramatically in the carved crucifix on the roodloft where the sight of Jesus on the cross, with Mary and John on either side, served as a powerful reminder of the central mystery of the Christian gospel.

It is all too easy to romanticize the mediaeval era, and one can hardly doubt that in the church, as indeed in the community at large from which it was inseparable, ignorance and superstition were rife. Yet it is impossible to locate any other period of Christian history when the communication of the gospel by means of the visual arts was taken so seriously or was so high in achievement. The reaction of the sixteenth-century Reformers against this proved to be so violent that the unity of faith and art was shattered beyond repair in many parts of Europe and, although the Baroque architecture and painting of Southern Europe in the seventeenth and eighteenth centuries was, and is, a source of inspiration in the years following the Reformation, it eventually lost touch with reality and ceased to edify.

Over nineteenth-century Christian art it seems kindest to draw a discreet veil and, while the present century has produced a little good glass and a few good paintings, it would be a brave man who could suggest in 1972 that the remaining years of the century might see a revival of interest and inspiration in this field of Christian communication. At this point I feel obliged to confess to a singular lack of valour.

## Drama

The churchman of the fourteenth century found instruction and edification not only in the examples of static art which surrounded him, but also in the mystery and morality plays which had by this time become an established feature in the life of parish churches. Performed by local, or travelling, groups of actors, these plays were extremely popular and frequently included a strong comic element. Angels climbed up and down from heaven on ladders, devils clad in bright clothes entered to claim the damned, sometimes an enterprising stage manager built a hell's mouth, designed to open and shut as Satan lured his victims to destruction. On a rather more cheerful note, many plays portrayed in outline the lives of saints, again with the use of elaborate properties, and also aspects of the Christian year. Here the nativity play at Christmas and the passion play during Holy Week were of special importance and when the weather conditions were favourable plays were often performed in the open air. The Corpus Christi outdoor procession normally included highly elaborate representations of the gospel stories and involved the participation of a large proportion of a village congregation. During the fifteenth and sixteenth centuries morality plays, in which a particular moral truth was communicated through characters who personified different virtues, became very popular. *Everyman* was the best known of these plays.

The popularity of the mediaeval plays and the skilful use made of them as channels of communication must not, however, lead us to suppose that they sprang from a long history of Christian drama. On the contrary, drama played no part in the life of the early church, and was in fact denounced by Tertullian in 200, then by Cyprian during the middle of the third century and again by Chrysostom in the fourth century. The reasons for their abhorrence of drama are not difficult to find. In the Roman world the *spectacula* had strong pagan associations and were usually replete with obscenity. Even non-Christians made public protests about this from time to time and a church which taught the virtue of asceticism could find no place in its life for anything remotely resembling the drama of the time.

All this came to an end with the fall of the Roman Empire, and the following centuries tell the fascinating story of how mediaeval drama slowly developed from the Christian liturgy. The dramatic elements in the Mass were there from the beginning, since the breaking of the bread was always conceived in terms of an action in which the words played a secondary, though obviously important, part. As the way in which the Mass was celebrated became more elaborate and formal, so the dramatic character of the liturgy became even more apparent and this was particularly so in the churches of the Gallican rite. Almalarius of Metz interpreted the Mass in dramatic terms at the beginning of the ninth century and St Ethelwold, who was Bishop of Winchester in the tenth century, spoke of 'the praiseworthy custom' of celebrating the death and resurrection of Christ by means of a mime and dialogue which might be performed either during or after the liturgy. In the same century a Saxony nun, Hrosvit, who was a considerable poetess, wrote several comedies with a religious slant but it is not clear whether these were ever performed before their discovery and printing in the early sixteenth century.

The bridge between ritual and representational drama was provided in the tenth century by *Quem Quaeritis*, a dramatic representation of the resurrection which began to find a place in the liturgy on Easter Day. Simple in concept, and exceedingly dramatic in its effect when well performed, *Quem Quaeritis* became the model for all subsequent plays in churches, and the cycle of the Christian year provided the stimulus and opportunity for further development. The close links with the liturgy were retained for another century, but when William Fitzstephen wrote of the popularity of religious drama in London's churches at the end of the twelfth century it appears that the plays had by this time become separated from the liturgy and the way was open for the mediaeval plays which retained a basic religious content, while not dependent upon the liturgy for their setting.

By the early part of the seventeenth century, however, the days of religious drama were virtually ended. John Wycliffe's followers had already foreshadowed the attitude of the Reformers when, in the late fourteenth century, they had declared the church plays to

44

be a violation of God's law and an obstacle to Christian belief. There was no room for apparent frivolity in the strict regimes inaugurated by Luther and Calvin and even though the Church of England was not attracted by extremes its new canons, promulgated in 1603, ruled that plays were not to be performed in churches. Hence the way was opened for the development of the secular theatre and the removal from the church's influence of one of the most powerful means of communication. There is sad irony in the fact that, while the student of drama traces the development of the contemporary theatre back to the liturgical *Quem Quaeritis*, the church has still to recognize a truth enunciated by Goethe: 'The highest cannot be spoken, it can only be acted.' The latest canons of the Church of England permit plays in churches but counsel caution and enjoin obedience to episcopal directives concerning choice and performance. This is a slight improvement on the situation during the previous three centuries, but is hardly the atmosphere in which religious drama is likely to flourish and one may wonder how well-qualified the majority of bishops are to pass judgment on the suitability or otherwise of the work of contemporary playwrights.

## Dancing

Although A. D. Nock declared, in an often-quoted statement, that 'primitive religion is not believed; it is danced', there is little historical precedent in the Christian tradition for the recent performance by the Royal Ballet in Coventry Cathedral or the danced Mass which featured among the festivities connected with the consecration of the new Roman Catholic Cathedral of Christ the King in Liverpool. Which is not to say that there has never been dancing in churches before. There is evidence of dancing during the fourth century, but the evidence comes from condemnations of the practice issued by bishops and councils. If the early church perceived danger in Roman drama, it is not altogether surprising that it frowned on Roman dancing. But people are not always obedient to bishops or councils, especially when the machinery for enforcing rules is somewhat rusty, and it seems

45

that dancing in churches persisted in some parts of Europe from the sixth to the ninth century.

It must not be supposed, however, that the dancing had any special liturgical associations or was ever thought of as a means of communication. It was no more, and no less, than the spontaneous expression of a festive spirit, felt by some Christians at joyful seasons of the church calendar. The Feast of Fools, celebrated with great zest and imagination in many parts of Europe and in some places in Britain from the twelfth to the fourteenth century, provided plenty of opportunity for dancing but this was still contrary to the wishes of bishops and was never officially recognized as a legitimate part of the church's life. The only exception to this is to be found in a few places where there was a tradition that after the celebration of his first Mass a newly ordained priest would dance with his mother.

Needless to say, the Reformers of the sixteenth and seventeenth centuries saw no place for dancing in either the church or secular society, and once fixed pews were installed in parish churches the scope for movement of any kind was considerably reduced. Here again, however, exceptions must be noted, for there is some evidence of Morris dancing in post-Reformation churches in England, and no one who has been in Seville during the feasts of Corpus Christi and the Immaculate Conception is likely to forget the dance of Los Seises, during which choirboys in mediaeval costumes dance before the reserved sacrament in the cathedral to the accompaniment of castanets. This tradition is said to go back to the fifteenth century.

From this it will be seen that the church has never regarded dancing as a legitimate form of communication, though one cannot close this section without reference to a comment by Sydney Carter at a London press conference held in connection with some dance arrangements which he had provided for a Eucharist in Southwark Cathedral. When asked by a reporter whether it was not unusual for dancing to take place around a Christian altar, Sydney Carter replied quite calmly: 'No, it has been happening for centuries, but the choreography has been rather poor.'

*Music*

Music, with or without the accompaniment of words, has always played an important part in Christian communication. The New Testament itself contains fragments of hymns, and Mark's account of the Last Supper tells us that after the meal Jesus and the apostles sang a hymn. By the third century one writer could refer to 'psalms and odes such as from the beginning were written by believers, hymns to the Christ, the Word of God, calling him God'. In the East, the hymns nearly always had a marked doctrinal emphasis, and in the West St Ambrose, who had a considerable influence on the development of music in worship, was particularly concerned about the doctrinal content of hymns. Those who sometimes feel anxious about the words of many of our Victorian hymns stand in a long tradition. The mixture of dogma and emotion which is powerfully expressed through music and singing is easily distorted or diluted so that whatever is communicated is barely recognizable as Christian. The Arian heresy was, we are told, propagated through the songs of boatmen and it was doubtless a widespread concern about the content of many hymns which led the Council of Braga (563) to decree that only biblical material might be used in the church's singing. A thousand years later, Calvin also laid down that only the words of scripture could be used in worship; hence the appearance, for better or for worse, of the metrical psalms.

Throughout Christian history the gospel has inspired some musicians to the highest peaks of creativity, while others have been lowered to the depths of banality. Which suggests that music is one of the most accurate and powerful means of communication open to the human race. Curiously, the Church of England's Book of Common Prayer makes virtually no provision for hymn singing, or indeed music of any kind, but according to the preface of the Methodist Hymn Book 'Methodism was born in song', and when one comes to inspect the vast output of the early Methodist leaders it is difficult to believe there was any hour of the day or night when they and their followers were not singing. By the beginning of the twentieth century churchmen had evidently had their fill of new hymns, but after a lull of some fifty years we now appear to be entering a new phase of creativity in this field, chiefly as a result of the pioneering efforts of Geoffrey Beaumont and Sydney Carter, who have helped the contemporary church to see that it need not remain cribbed and confined by the limitations of Victorian hymnody.

The real problem now, as always, is the extent to which the use of poetic imagery, essential in hymn writing, may distort the beliefs of those who use them, particularly during their early formative years. The fact that a considerable number of Englishmen believe God to be remote from ordinary life and experience is not due to their close attention to the Bible or to preaching but to childhood memories of singing 'There's a friend for little children above the bright blue sky.' Whether the author of that hymn believed God to inhabit outer space, or was simply using graphic poetic imagery, the consequences are the same. A close examination of the words of many Victorian hymns, which still form the staple diet of music in the majority of British churches, will disclose almost every heresy condemned by the church down the centuries, besides many others that bishops and theologians have never even dreamt of. If these hymns were simply expressing the beliefs and aspirations of an individual, presumably the writer, this would hardly matter. A bit of heresy has never done anyone any harm. But when words which are not only heretical but positively misleading become one of the church's primary channels of communication it is surely time to take notice. There is something absurd about taking infinite pains over every word in a credal statement or a liturgical prayer, while caring nothing for the words in the hymn book. Without wishing to suggest narrow, or even very clearly-defined, boundaries of belief, I feel that the time has certainly come for a drastic purging of our hymn books. This is sensitive territory. Some will argue that the singers of hymns take little notice of the words; others that the good will eventually drive out the bad. But if the words are of little importance the value of hymn-singing itself seems to be called in question, and the experience of the past hundred years suggests that bad hymns are endowed with remarkable staying power. The answer to the problem is not of course censorship, which would in any case be impossible to enforce, but a closer working relationship between the artist and the reflective theologian so that each may benefit from the other's insights and skills.

Significantly, while the church has been floundering in the field of contemporary music, a number of composers and songwriters involved in the great musical explosion of pop, rock, folk and blues which began in the early 1960s have turned to religious themes. The results may not have been to the taste of many churchgoers, but an examination of the words of many of the most popular songs reveals a good deal of theology and deep insight into human needs and aspirations. If the church continues to ignore this phenomenon it will be turning its back on the most powerful means of communication at work in the world of today's young people. Most recently, we have seen the development of the individual item into full-length musicals, like *Jesus Christ Superstar* and *Godspell*, which are productions of the highest order and are making a considerable impact on the large audiences which they attract. In an appreciative review of *Godspell*, Harold Hobson, the distinguished *Sunday Times* theatre critic, went as far as to compare it with Handel's *Messiah*; the only difference in approach he could discern was that one was written in the eighteenth century, and the other in the twentieth.

## Unexplored territories

Having tried to survey, in an absurdly brief compass, the broad direction taken by the church in various fields of communication over the centuries, it is now necessary to point to some other fields on which Christian communicators have hardly ventured but which will demand attention in the not so far distant future.

The first concerns those aspects of non-verbal communication which involve a serious consideration of the place of the body, in particular the sense of touch. Members of the Esalen community in California have already reminded us that, whether we like it or not, we are already involved in a good deal of non-verbal communication. They go on to insist that this should not only be recognized but positively encouraged, and that we should

49

acknowledge the unity of body, mind and spirit by greater use of our bodies in the expression of feelings and emotions. Since the churches have over the years made considerable use in worship of such actions as laying-on-of-hands, joining-of-hands, prostration, kneeling and the kiss of peace they are hardly in a strong position to argue against the Esalen thesis. Whether they are prepared to move beyond the traditional actions and gestures is, however, another matter, but the challenge to develop what some American writers are pleased to call 'a visceral theology' cannot be ignored by those who take the incarnation seriously.

The second field of enquiry takes us into the new approach to communication pioneered by the Canadian Marshall McLuhan. He argues that until the invention of printing the primary means of communication was speech, which is inevitably random and discontinuous. Printing changed this, however, and imposed upon mankind a highly organized, 'linear' form of communication which has proved to be socially divisive since only a certain number of people, the 'inner-directed', can cope with the type of discipline involved. The development of the 'electric media' – radio and, especially, television – has now changed the situation. No longer are we at the mercy of the logical and the orderly; we have returned to the random and the spontaneous. This, combined with the facility for transmitting information to every part of the world instantaneously, has provided the basis for a new solidarity among the inhabitants of our 'global village'. Furthermore, argues McLuhan, the revolution has brought us to recognize that the important factor in communication is not what we read or what we see, but that we actually read and actually see; 'The medium is the message.' It is by no means easy to grapple with McLuhan's thinking, and any suggestion of infallibility concerning his analysis needs to be resisted, but his approach demands the most serious consideration – not least by a church which, for the greater part of its life, survived with but little recourse to the written word and owes its origin to an event in which the Word became flesh – not print.

# 4 The Written Word

As we have seen, the churches have, since the Gutenberg revolution, made valiant attempts to harness the written word to the communication of the Christian faith. And though the main thesis of this book is that too much emphasis has been, and still is being, placed on the verbalizing of the gospel, it cannot be denied that the written word continues to play an important part in all work of communication and that its full potential has still to be exploited by the churches.

The Bible remains a best seller and there is a ready market for the apparently unending flow of twentieth-century translations. Societies such as the Bible Reading Fellowship and the Scripture Union publish vast quantities of notes designed to encourage individuals to regular Bible reading and to some understanding of what they read. But it is difficult to assess how many of the Bibles are read and how widely the notes are actually used. Those in touch with Christian groups other than of an evangelical tradition are not normally impressed by the degree of biblical knowledge displayed by the membership. On the contrary, it is safer for anyone wishing to introduce a discussion on any part of the Bible to assume that his companions are virtually ignorant of the text or have only an incomplete or inaccurate knowledge of a particular incident or story; this notwithstanding the fact that the Bible has provided the main diet of religious education in schools for more than a century.

Given this situation in regard to the Bible, no one will be surprised to learn that it is quite unusual to meet a Christian who has read more than a handful of books which might be categorized as religious or theological. A poll might well reveal that the majority of Christians have never read one such book, and those responsible for the manning of church bookstalls will testify to the difficulty they experience in selling their wares and the monotonous regularity with which they record an annual financial loss and a mounting stock of dog-eared literature. The Christian is evidently less ready to read about the faith and the church than the fishing enthusiast is ready to read about rivers and their contents, and the do-it-yourself man about the methods and materials available for home improvement.

Part of the reason for this is undoubtedly to be found in the exceedingly low standard of much 'popular' religious writing in the present century and the apparent inability of scholars to communicate their knowledge and insights in forms which the non-professional reader might understand. A theological library is one of the dullest places on earth and there is surely something quite alarming about a situation in which those who endeavour to communicate their experience of the living God can do no more than present him as a crashing old bore. But low standards and technical language are not the only explanation of the rampant theological illiteracy. There is a peculiar national factor involved, which comes to light when it is realized that Scottish and American churchmen are not so reluctant to take a theological book into their hands, even though the levels of technicality and banality are on the whole much higher in the religious literature of both these countries. The Englishman is essentially pragmatic in his approach to religious matters. He is, with some justification, exceedingly suspicious of doctrinal formulation and of the speculative thought which flows from this source. It is no accident that such distinctive beliefs as the Church of England possesses are to be discovered only through the use of the Book of Common Prayer. Methodists turn to their hymn book for doctrine and inspiration, and though the churches which now constitute the United Reformed Church have quite distinct theological roots in history they resort but infrequently to their classical confessions of faith and are normally embarrassed when they do so.

This position is, however, changing and there is no better symbol of the change than Bishop John Robinson's *Honest to God*. Conceived as a modest contribution to a theological discussion in which students were interested, the publisher planned paperback sales of 10,000 copies in Britain and North America. In the event, well over a million copies (in seventeen different languages) have now been sold. No other religious work, apart from the Bible itself, has ever achieved such a wide circulation.

Leaving on one side certain special, and it appears unrepeatable, factors which contributed to the success of *Honest to God*, it is possible to discern two other elements in the book which have significance for those who are involved in religious publishing. The first of these is concerned with a new interest in the intellectual basis of the Christian faith. Although the Englishman may not be very interested in theology as it has been traditionally presented, he is not unaware that the changes in the intellectual climate of the past century have posed a challenge to religious belief. He feels this in his bones and, as his own intellectual attainments rise, the challenge becomes a personal one. *Honest to God* recognized this and uncorked a bottle which was sooner or later bound to explode. The second, equally important, factor is that Bishop Robinson was able to write attractively and personally. Unlike the majority of those called to high office in the church, he is a gifted writer who can range from the academic treatise to pages of a tabloid newspaper. Some careful scholars complained that *Honest to God* was 'muddled', but a little confusion seems a small price to pay for one who can introduce the thought of Bonhoeffer, Bultmann and Tillich to those standing in the market place.

The personal factor was also significant. Bishop Robinson wrote his book as an expression of his own agonizing about the meaning of faith and out of direct experience of responsibility for Christian communication in one of the most intractable mission areas in Britain. Professor Christopher Evans was right when he said, in a broadcast review, that the proper place for *Honest to God* in his library was in the section reserved for books of personal devotion. The element of personal honesty, evidently rare in a bishop's public image, played no small part in arousing interest in this particular book.

Recognizing that there are unlikely to be any more *Honest to*

*God*s, it is nonetheless reasonable to assume that there will be a continuing and growing market for books of a non-academic character which are dealing with important issues in the realm of religious faith, which are written attractively and bear the stamp of personal integrity. The experience of publishing houses on both sides of the Atlantic bears this out, even though the problems of publishing any form of literature are infinitely greater than they were just a decade ago.

These problems, mainly economic, now make it impossible for the churches to contribute very much through their own publishing houses. The recent demise of the Carey Kingsgate Press (Baptist) and Burns and Oates (Roman Catholic), and the present difficulties of the SPCK (Anglican) and the Epworth Press (Methodist) are symptoms of a general trend in the publishing world. This demands that the scale of operations should be large enough to function economically and to exploit a wide and diverse market. In turn, the publisher can only consider manuscripts which are likely to appeal to a fairly large readership or are sufficiently significant to attract the attention of libraries.

While this development may preclude the discovery of a few writers who need the support of a small publishing house in order to find their literary feet, the overall benefits should more than outweigh this loss. The more careful selection of manuscripts for publication should lead to a raising of standards in religious book publishing – though the temptation to produce popular trash will be stronger – and the employment of large-scale and highly professional marketing techniques is already placing religious books in shops where they had hitherto not been available. Professor Martin E. Marty of Chicago was perhaps overstating the case when he once told me that the best index to the religious publishing trade was to be found by examining the racks of airport bookstalls, but he was making a valid point and if Christian writers are to be able to share their insights and experiences with a cross section of humanity their books must be available in the general bookshops and not restricted to specialist outlets in cathedral cities.

Having acknowledged this as a fact of contemporary life and a not undesirable development, a question remains concerning whether the churches themselves have any part to play in the future of religious publishing. On present evidence, the answer is yes. The churches have a number of domestic requirements which cannot be met by the large publishing houses, ranging from official reports to pamphlets and liturgical texts, and it may well be in their own interests to produce highly-specialized works or to encourage young writers who find it difficult to break into the wider publishing field.

In present circumstances, it seems highly unlikely that the British churches can support more than one such publishing venture between them and it seems certain that some form of subsidy will be necessary to keep it in existence during the remaining years of the present century. Whether the churches will be ready to co-operate at this level and produce funds for the purpose will, naturally, depend on the importance they attach to the printed word as a medium for the expression of the Christian faith. One may only hope that it may be regarded as at least as important as many other pieces of ecclesiastical activity which are costly to maintain.

A responsibility also rests with the churches over the all-important question of book-selling. The major publishing houses advertise their wares, some of which are reviewed in the religious and secular press, but if the ordinary layman is to become aware of particular books and buy them the local churches will have to play a much greater part than they have done in calling attention to books of special interest and making them easily available. As I have already indicated, general bookstalls in churches are notoriously difficult to maintain, except in large centres of population, but if a certain book is recommended by the priest or minister, and copies of it are available in church, laypeople are nearly always ready to buy a few. Similarly, when books provide the material for study groups and other educational exercises there is rarely any difficulty in obtaining purchasers.

Most churches have hardly begun to make use of the paperback explosion and the very considerable resources available for an outlay of 50p or less. There is of course no obligation on anyone to keep the wolf from the publisher's door, or to come to the rescue of ailing church publishing houses, but effective Christian communication requires that the best books should be more widely circulated and more skilfully used.

If this is true of the world of books, what can be said of the church press? Here one enters a world of unbelievable gloom and tottering foundations. No one who has not been required to devote every Friday morning to reading the weekly church papers can begin to understand how appalling they are. It may be argued of course that these papers simply reflect the condition of the bodies they are seeking to serve, but if this were so it is difficult to see how the churches continue to exist. In fairness to those who produce them it must be said at once that they are starved of resources and are generally working under conditions which no secular journalist would tolerate for more than a few minutes. But even if these things were remedied one is left with the distinct impression that lack of vision is the chief problem. The church press should serve not only as a mirror but also as a source of insight and an instrument for change.

In terms of circulation, and of competence at the production level, the Roman Catholic journals occupy the most prominent position. Here it must be noted that it is far from easy to discover the circulation figures of any of the church newspapers. For reasons best known to themselves – and therefore highly suspect – most refuse to publish audited figures, but we may perhaps assume that if any of the papers had a dramatic increase in circulation this fact would not go unrecorded. In the meantime we will be content with approximate figures which help to paint a general picture.

The two Roman Catholic popular weeklies, *The Universe* and the *Catholic Herald*, are unique in that more than 90% of their sales are effected at church doors, i.e. to worshippers leaving Mass. Having suggested that the sale of books ought to be encouraged in churches, it may appear to be a trifle inconsistent to highlight the dangers of church door sales for newspapers, yet these are so real, and so pernicious, that they cannot be overlooked. The price of the high circulations made possible by this effective form of distribution has to be paid in the coinage of what amounts to censorship by the local parish priest.

Editors of all journals are well aware that they cannot please all the readers all the time, and that some will stop buying the paper if they disagree with a particular editorial stance. All being well, these individual defections will be offset by the recruitment of new readers, and the overall circulation maintained. The story is, however, somewhat different when the channels of distribution become closed. A parish priest who takes exception to the editorial line of one of the Catholic weeklies may not only cease to purchase the paper himself; he may also decide that it ought not to be sold at his church door, thus depriving the editor of as many as 300 readers at one blow.

That this is neither a remote possibility nor an insignificant factor in Catholic journalism may be seen by examining Desmond Fisher's editorship of the *Catholic Herald* during the years immediately following Vatican II. Almost certainly the most able journalist in the religious field in the past two decades, Fisher was deeply influenced by the spirit of Vatican II and, not surprisingly, this found expression in the pages of his paper. But Fisher was too far ahead of those holding the reins of power in English Catholicism. He urged reforms which they were not ready to accept or implement. He was bold enough to criticize members of the hierarchy who were dragging their feet or still ventilating ideas current in the pre-Conciliar era. At once he came under pressure to observe the canons of 'loyalty' and to cease 'rocking the ship'. A rumour that Cardinal Heenan was involved and had addressed a letter on the subject to the directors of the *Catholic Herald* was promptly denied by Archbishop's House, but there was ample evidence that the Cardinal's disquiet had reached the ears of the management, if not by official correspondence, then by equally efficient channels. Soon afterwards Desmond Fisher departed. His editorship had been bold and imaginative, but the directors were able to point to declining circulation and, in fact, the company responsible for printing the paper had to undertake a financial rescue operation by assuming a majority shareholding in the enterprise. Since then the *Catholic Herald* has pursued an editorial policy of such a moderate character that it is rarely possible to discern whether its successive editors, Desmond Albrow and Gerard Noel, hold any opinions at all. A mixture of news reporting, features, reviews and voluminous readers' correspondence is presented in modern newspaper format and the circulation, which continues to fluctuate, round about 90,000.

Competing with the *Catholic Herald*, and always a serious threat to its survival, is *The Universe*. Until recently an important part of the Burns and Oates publishing empire, *The Universe* has for many years served as the house journal of Catholic folk religion. Its loyalty to authority, papal or episcopal, has never been in doubt. If the Pope declared the moon to be made of green cheese, the editor of *The Universe* would be among the first to agree and, for good measure, might well publish a picture of a nun gazing into the heavens in acknowledgment of the new revelation. The readers of this attractively produced tabloid, which is now making extensive use of colour, are left in no doubt that their allegiance is to the 'one true church' and although authority sometimes decrees ecumenical activity this is reported grudgingly and, on occasion, offensively. As a channel of communication within English Catholicism (there is also a Scottish edition) *The Universe* is of considerable importance. A decline in circulation from the 300,000 to the 250,000 mark caused the ownership to be transferred to the Liverpool Daily Post in the late 1960s, but the fact that it is greatly despised by Catholic intellectuals posits no threat to its survival, in the short term. It will be interesting to see how, and whether, the paper evolves to meet the new demands of a better educated Catholic laity. In the long term, its survival will depend on flexibility at this point.

Before leaving the Roman Catholic scene, it is necessary to take note of *The Tablet*, an old-established weekly for intellectuals which once enjoyed a very high reputation in literary circles and still has aspirations in this direction. Its most valuable feature in recent years has been several pages of overseas news and documentation of important pronouncements and decrees from Rome. The general standard of writing and reviewing is high, an increasing amount of space is allocated to secular subjects and the re-designing of the magazine's layout at the beginning of 1972 brought *The Tablet* to a leading position in contemporary religious journalism. The main complaint against the journal is its right-wing political stance, expressed consistently in editorials penned, one might guess, by former British diplomats who gather in a London club to settle the future of the world and the church over a bottle of brandy. Whether *The Tablet* will survive seems doubtful. Its circulation, in the region of 12,000, was showing an upward trend during the early months of 1972 but the accounts still show a deficit and the magazine no longer has the protection of *The Universe*, in whose bosom it formerly sheltered and some of whose profits it conveniently absorbed. While the present editor and owner, Tom Burns, has sufficient interest and funds to keep it going, it will undoubtedly continue, but he is not a young man and it is difficult to see how a magazine of such a size and so limited a circulation can survive unaided in the present economic climate. Its demise would be a serious blow to religious journalism in Britain and, although *The Tablet* has few friends among the hierarchy, it is to be hoped that someone in authority will recognize its importance sufficiently to ensure that it continues for many more years as an independent journal in which intelligent Catholics may air their views and be kept abreast of developments in the church as a whole.

Within the Church of England the *Church Times* is the main channel of communication. Often regarded as a joke in clerical circles, it is nevertheless read by most Anglican clergymen who like to keep in touch with what is happening outside their own parishes, who are greatly interested in the weekly list of appointments and, in the summer months, show a certain concern for the Church Times Cricket Cup competition. Basically the house journal of a clerical trade union, it reaches out to a certain number of laity and the general standard of reporting and presentation is high. Unfortunately, the editorial opinion frequently displays Christianity in a scarcely recognizable form and evokes from readers some of the worst elements in human nature. In the vitriol stakes, the *Church Times* has few equals in any sphere of journalism. Even so, it performs a very useful function for the

Church of England and, as its editor and owner pointed out to the English bishops in the summer of 1970, the survival of the newspaper must in the not so long run depend on much stronger support (i.e. sales) from its constituency.

How it will secure this support is far from easy to see. Bishops may exhort their dioceses to show greater interest, but this will not sell many more copies, and the *Church Times* itself obviously lacks the resources to engage in large-scale promotion campaigns. The majority of the clergy, while ready to purchase a copy themselves, do not feel it would provide a wholesome diet for the layman (which is perfectly true) and so the circulation declines by 2,000 every year as retirement and death take their toll of regular readers. Now below 50,000 sales per week, there is no reason to suppose that G. J. Palmer & Sons will keep the paper in existence once it moves into the red, nor is there any reason why they should.

The outlook for the Church of England in the field of weekly journalism is therefore far from healthy. The *Church of England Newspaper*, now part of the Christian Weekly Newspapers Group, commands little support, except in evangelical circles and its contents are as unattractive as its appearance. Subsidized by Sir Alfred Owen and other right-wing political interests, there were indications in 1968 that further money would not be forthcoming if the then editor, John King, continued to annoy the more conservative elements of the evangelical wing. The problem was solved by the departure of King and the appointment of a more 'reliable' editorial team. In 1970 it absorbed the ailing *British Weekly* and now appears in three separate editions, each containing a certain amount of common feature material but with news coverage geared to particular Anglican and Free Church interests. It is too early to say whether this will lead to long-term financial viability, but a considerable improvement in content will be needed before the prospects of its demise will cause much alarm. The combined circulation of the three editions, named individually as the *Church of England Newspaper*, the *British Weekly* and the *Christian Record*, is now about 43,000.

Perhaps the healthiest, financially, of all the church weeklies is the *Baptist Times*. Its aims are extremely limited – to serve as the house organ of the Baptist Union – and it is run on a shoe-string, but it has 18,000 loyal purchasers and the combination of low running costs with this circulation gives it a stability which other editors doubtless envy. The price in terms of journalism is, however, heavy for the *Baptist Times* is easily the dullest of the church weeklies and the one most closely tied to denominational apron strings. Its reports of Baptist Union Council meetings (to which its reporters alone are admitted) are subject to official scrutiny before publication and editorial criticism of Council policy is unheard of. When the chairman of the Council resigned in late 1970 over a controversial theological paper delivered by Principal Michael Taylor at the annual assembly of that year, the announcement was given the minimum of coverage on an inside page and, after the General Secretary had issued an appeal for unity in the denomination, discussion of the theological issues in the paper's correspondence columns was abruptly closed.

The other major Free Church weekly, the *Methodist Recorder*, also has a loyalty to its denomination which many journalists regard with suspicion and which offends against those canons of journalism concerned with freedom. Although it is owned by an independent company, a number of leading members of the Methodist hierarchy are closely involved in policy making and it echoes with great accuracy the official viewpoint of the central departments, as those who have tried to voice criticisms in its columns know to their cost. The most flagrant and revealing instance of dependence was seen in 1970 after the announcement of the grants to African freedom fighting movements by the World Council of Churches. The news from Geneva arrived in London shortly before the *Recorder*'s printing deadline and the editor was required to compose a hasty editorial on the subject. This he did, expressing grave concern at the WCC's action. But during the ensuing days it appeared that the Methodist leadership, showing commendable courage in a company of otherwise dithering English churchmen, was firmly committed to support of the World Council. Result: an editorial in the next week's

*Recorder* backing the grants to freedom fighters. But while the paper contains a certain amount of normally well-informed political comment, the overwhelming emphasis is on the internal life of Methodism and, in spite of the many changes both within and without the church during the past half century, it remains the kind of journal which a secure and respectable nonconformist family might have read between church services on any Sunday in the 1920s. Unfortunately, the number of secure and respectable Methodist families is declining, and so is the *Recorder*'s circulation, but it still sells between 50,000 and 60,000 copies a week and can count on the loyalty of Methodism's local lay leadership. The danger to the *Recorder*, as to the *Church Times*, is not of dramatic collapse but of steady erosion. A loss of 2,000 readers a year is not significant in itself, but when the loss totals 10,000 in five years problems begin to arise over advertising revenue, and a loss of 20,000 in ten years may well cause the whole edifice to crack. The future for these papers is therefore far from bright.

Of the other denominational journals, mention must be made of *The Friend*, a modest Quaker weekly which faithfully reflects the ethos and interests of the Society of Friends and is, therefore, the most secular and least aggressive of the church papers. The *Congregational Monthly* and *Outlook* (Presbyterian) are monthlies, serving fairly small constituencies, well produced and, without ever reaching the lofty heights of excitement, rarely insulting the intelligences of their readers. In this field one must be thankful for small mercies. They will combine in the autumn of 1972 to provide a journal for the new United Reformed Church.

The overall picture of the church press is, therefore, of a variety of journals occupying common ground in that their primary concerns are ecclesiastical and firmly denominational. As channels of communication within the churches they enjoy limited success since only the Roman Catholic weeklies reach a significant proportion of the church membership. Not one of them would be suitable for placing in the hands of anyone who was not already deeply committed to the church. It would be prudent to keep all of them out of the sight of intelligent enquirers about the Christian faith.

In an attempt to improve on this depressing situation, the Rev. Timothy Beaumont (now Lord Beaumont of Whitley) launched *New Christian* in 1965. The aim of his enterprise was to produce an ecumenical fortnightly paper, with a secular bias, which would be of service to what appeared at the time to be a growing radical/reforming movement in the churches and also appeal to people on the edge of the ecclesiastical organization, i.e. those just holding to their church commitment and those outside the church but concerned about Christian values and insights. Modelled on the secular weeklies, *New Christian* was built on the base provided by *Prism*, an Anglican monthly with a circulation of just under 3,000, and, as a result of a £10,000 promotion campaign, was selling 10,000 copies at the end of the first year. The readership was almost equally divided between clergy and laity, and between Anglicans and members of other churches. The initial objective was realized: the magazine attracted the interest of leading churchmen and politicians, as well as a fair number of people with no firm commitment to the church.

It soon became clear, however, that *New Christian* was faced with intractable financial problems. In order to break even, a circulation of 20,000–25,000 was required. Assuming that a potential market of this size existed, it was apparent that this could only be reached if the magazine became available through booksellers and newsagents, and if a considerable sum of money was spent on promotion. Neither proved possible. Owing to its modest beginnings, *New Christian* was unable to overcome the hurdle formed by the major magazine wholesalers, who believed it would not be profitable for them to handle, and the finance needed for heavy and continuous promotion was not available. After five years – during which the magazine attracted contributions from the best theological writers in the country and established an international reputation – it was necessary to call a halt and, in an effort to save something from the wreckage, *New Christian* was merged with the long established American weekly, *The Christian Century*. The British churches owe a considerable debt of gratitude to Lord Beaumont of Whitley, who spent a very large amount of money on *New Christian* and provided a fleeting glimpse of the kind of religious journal which might be of service in the closing decades of the twentieth century.

A further lesson is to be learned from the *New Christian* experience. If the churches wish to move into new spheres of religious journalism they will have to operate ecumenically and also be prepared to provide financial subsidies. It is not difficult to criticize the denominational weeklies and this chapter has not attempted to cover up their deficiencies. But those of us who worked on *New Christian* were aware that we were in a highly privileged position in that we were able to draw on the theological and literary resources of all the churches. Unlike the denominational papers, which had largely to confine themselves to contributors from the churches they served, *New Christian* could seek and receive work from the most creative writers in any church – and also from outside the church. Competition for space was so keen that it proved possible to publish only one in ten of the unsolicited articles submitted for consideration.

The question of subsidies is a difficult one, since those who pay the piper normally wish to call the tune. We have already noticed that the close attachment of certain denominational papers to their churches results in a somewhat feeble product, even when there are no financial strings. The secular press, which is facing similar financial problems to those of the religious press (though obviously on a much larger scale), is resistant to the suggestion of government subsidies for newspapers, though the majority of daily newspapers are in fact heavily subsidized in one form or another from commercial sources. Yet it is clear that if Britain is to continue to have a reasonable choice of newspapers there will in the end have to be state subsidy of some kind since readers cannot (for a variety of reasons – some good, some bad) be persuaded to pay the full cost of production.

The churches might well pioneer the new trail. A consortium could be formed to take control of the *Catholic Herald*, the *Church Times*, the *Church of England Newspaper*, the *British Weekly*, the *Methodist Recorder*, and the *Baptist Times*. If we are in an optimistic mood, we are entitled to hope that the present owners of these papers would be prepared to relinquish control quite soon, having been properly compensated for the value of their property. If we are pessimistic, we must be prepared to wait patiently for the papers to reach the borders of bankruptcy before they can become involved in the project, but obviously it is desirable to begin from a position of relative strength.

A board would then be established consisting of people in the following categories: (1) representatives of the participating churches with skills in theology, politics, sociology, etc; (2) experienced newspaper executives; (3) journalists. Those representing the churches would not be drawn from the ranks of the ecclesiastical bureaucrats and their professional skills would be the primary factor in their nomination. They would receive part-time salaries. The business executives and journalists would be nominated solely on the basis of their skills.

The consortium would be set up for an initial period of ten years and guaranteed such financial support as was needed for the launching and development of the project. The board would be left entirely free to appoint its own editorial staff and, while the staff would be expected to consult the board over broad lines of policy, they would in turn be free to conduct the affairs of the journals in accordance with their own ideas and skills. Obviously, there are risks involved in this arrangement. A considerable sum of money might well be involved in a ten-year programme, but the readiness of the participating churches to commit themselves for a decade and face a considerable loss would be an important test of their seriousness in undertaking the project. On the other hand, a period of less than ten years would be unrealistic for the breaking of new ground and the financial implications would not be heavy when considered in the light of the churches' expenditure in other fields. Again, the almost complete autonomy granted to the board and to the editorial staff would not be easy for the churches to contemplate, but only by giving this freedom would the project have public credibility and the journalists the proper conditions in which to exercise their skills.

The publishing programme would involve the production of two journals: a weekly newspaper designed for the ordinary church membership, and a fortnightly review designed for the clergy and those laity who had had some form of higher education. The chief ingredient in the newspaper would be news, but there would be features, editorial comment and reviews. An initial circulation of 300,000 would not be an unreasonable expectation and this could rise dramatically if editorial content and promotion schemes were attractive; the churches still have a sizeable constituency which has not yet been tested with a reasonable product. The fortnightly review might expect to begin with a circulation of about 15,000 and aim for a target of about 35,000.

Two journals of this kind would, with imaginative and skilful direction, be of great service to the churches and stand a very good chance of achieving financial viability. The parallels with other aspects of the ecumenical movement are obvious: the sharing of resources leads to the better deployment of talent and the more responsible stewardship of money. Of course, no one should pretend that the operation would be easy and without risk. But what are the alternatives, apart from the lingering death of the existing church papers and the total loss of a potentially important channel of communication? A good test of the quality of the two projected journals would be whether or not they might be placed in the hands of a non-churchman without embarrassment. The ecumenical parallels are again obvious.

Minor, but not insignificant, experiments are already taking place in this field at the local level. As the financial problems attendant upon the publishing of parish and congregational magazines become more acute, and the achievement of reasonable editorial standards more difficult, groups of churches in towns and rural areas are finding the way to salvation by means of joint magazines and newspapers. Where this has happened, the result is nearly always to be seen in a journal which achieves professional standards of production, has a stimulating editorial content and a small balance in the bank.

The chief problem with these local journals is securing continuity of editorship. They are normally the brain child of an enthusiastic and gifted individual who, sooner or later, moves away from the area, leaving an empty, or inadequately filled, editorial chair behind him. If, however, communication by means of the printed word is ever recognized as an important part of the church's work it is not unreasonable to expect that the number of local, ecumenical journals will increase and the pool of skilled editors be enlarged. Even at the present time, the skills of Christian journalists are not being fully utilized in the production of good local papers or in the training of future editors.

Apart from joint enterprises of this kind, it now appears that most local churches will in future be able to publish little more than a newsletter for circulation within congregations and to others on the fringe of the church. Insets for incorporation into local magazines continue to appear but they are now struggling against heavy odds, owing to increasing costs and declining circulations, and it is unlikely that they will survive the 1970s. A local newsletter is not, however, to be despised and may provide a useful channel of communication within a church community provided that its limitations are recognized. Costs are certain to remain a problem, but effective communication can hardly ever be achieved on the cheap and expenditure on communication ought not to be regarded as a luxury or an optional extra when church budgets are under consideration.

The greater part of this chapter has inevitably been taken up with an assessment of the possibilities open to the churches for Christian communication through those channels where they have considerable influence, if not actual control. In a situation where these channels are themselves subject to considerable change, because of external pressures, a change of strategy, or rather the beginning of a strategy, is a crying need. Yet the vast majority of those who will ever read a theological book or pick up a religious newspaper are likely to be people who already have some association with the church. How is the Christian experience to be shared, by means of the written word, with the rest of humanity? It can only be through the existing secular channels of communication.

In Britain, at the present time, the opportunities for doing this are still considerable. The 'quality' daily newspapers still feel that religion is important enough to justify the employment of a specialist reporter on church affairs and to allocate space for reporting and commenting on developments in the religious field. *The Guardian*, very properly, treats subjects and articles on their merits and is prepared to publish items which conform to the newspaper's own high standards of literacy and intelligence. *The Times*, evidently believing the churches to be part of the establishment which has to be represented in its columns, is less discriminating and allocates space on Saturdays and Mondays to theologians and preachers who are not always skilled in communicating on the Christian/secular frontier. Even so, the space is allocated on a regular basis and the feature pages also carry well-informed articles on religious (mainly Roman Catholic) subjects with some frequency. For many years, Dr W. R. Matthews has occupied a Saturday corner in *The Daily Telegraph* and this newspaper's coverage of church events is substantial, even if somewhat uneven.

The point here is that the more skilled Christian writers ought to be making greater efforts to get their work published in these secular organs which open up the possibility of communication with millions of people. If the subject is right and the writing attractive, there is a very good chance that the articles will find their way into print. Again, it must be emphasized that the aim is not infiltration for propaganda purposes – any writer with this in mind would almost certainly fail to produce anything acceptable to an editor – but simply to make a contribution to the current debate about the human condition. Christians have no special right to be heard, but they are entitled to make an effort to be heard and if they are prepared, or able, to make a contribution in terms which are meaningful to those who do not share their beliefs or experiences there are still quite a lot of thoughtful people ready to listen.

Moving into the realms of the 'popular' dailies raises different problems and is much less easy. Since this section of the press exists chiefly to provide its readers with entertainment, the opportunities for serious discussion of any subject are naturally somewhat limited, though the *Daily Mirror* has certain high ideals which ought not to be sneered at by anyone who is concerned with human welfare and which one would like to see translated more effectively in the lives of the churches. It is also a fact that the number of writers who can communicate at the level of the popular press is extremely limited, and the number of religious writers able to operate in this field almost negligible. Until such writers have emerged and offered their work to papers like *The Sun*, the *Daily Mail* and the *Daily Express* it is impossible to discover just how open is this territory. What can be said with confidence, however, is that few editors can resist a good article on a matter of real human concern and presented in such a way as to attract and hold the interest of their readers.

It is impossible in a book of this length to venture into the realm of the novel and discuss the work of Christian communication which has been, and is being, carried out by gifted writers who are sensitive to human needs and aspirations and are aware of the essentially mysterious character of human life. Suffice it to say that this is one of the most crucial channels of written Christian communication and, though novelists cannot be made to order, their work cannot be neglected by any community in whose foundation documents the parable plays so prominent a part.

# 5   The Spoken Word

The fact that verbal communication is only one of many different channels through which experience and insight is shared, and that undue emphasis has been placed on this channel at the expense of the rest, should not lead to an undervaluing of its place in the life of the Christian community. After all, such knowledge as we have of the life and teaching of Jesus owes its origin to an oral tradition. For many centuries, as we have seen, this was the chief way in which men and women conveyed to others what they had themselves learned of Christ. In every human relationship conversation has a crucial part to play, as we quickly discover if we find ourselves in a country or a group of people whose language we do not understand. Many of those at present outside the church are in a similar position: they have difficulty in comprehending what Christians are saying about their experience of God and their understanding of life. Some of this difficulty is inevitable, since the Christian seeks to articulate his experience of a mystery, but much of it is due to insensitivity to the way in which those outside the Christian tradition are able to receive information or insight concerning the religious dimension of life. Little thought has been given to this particular problem within the churches – a strange omission in bodies deeply committed to communicating to others what they have themselves received and experienced.

Those involved in religious broadcasting have not, however, been able to escape this discipline and though the early days of broadcasting saw excessive reliance on particular individuals who were 'natural' communicators, recent years have seen the development of considerable skill in the BBC's sound radio department. The real breakthrough came when it was decided, in the face of some opposition from churchmen, to substitute for the long-established Sunday evening service a programme which would allow a wide variety of approaches, including discussion, interview and drama. It was recognized that a sermon in the context of worship had serious limitations when transferred to the homes of those listeners (the overwhelming majority) who could not accept Christian presuppositions or understand much of the traditional Christian terminology. Opportunities for questioning and the expression of doubt were needed. Alternative methods of reflecting religious belief and practice were demanded by an age in which the traditional approach of the churches lay outside the experience of the general population.

At this point it is necessary to emphasize as strongly as possible that it is not the function of the BBC or the ITA to act as agencies for the propagation of the Christian faith, or indeed of any particular way of life. The purpose of broadcasting, in Britain at any rate, is to inform, to educate and to entertain. In times of national emergency it has been necessary to modify this function in order to serve a greater good, but in normal circumstances any suggestion that broadcasting should become an instrument of propaganda has, rightly, been firmly resisted. The fact that Christians may believe themselves to be in possession of certain important truths does not entitle them to occupy a privileged position in this respect and the debates about religious broadcasting which take place in official church assemblies from time to time would be more edifying and creative if this fact were more widely recognized.

Programmes with a religious content are broadcast because the Christian faith still informs a good deal of Britain's public life, because the churches have a significant place in the country's social institutions, and because a very large number of people have a Christian commitment or accept Christian values. If a situation ever arises when Britain is a secular state, in which its Christian heritage has been renounced or superceded, the case for religious broadcasting could no longer be made. This does not, however, appear to be an imminent possibility and, in the meantime, it is entirely proper that broadcasting should reflect and illuminate the religious situation as it now is. The presence in Britain of people from other countries who hold non-Christian beliefs also raises a question concerning the reflection of their interests in religious broadcasting, and this can only be decided in the light of their numbers and influence in the life of the nation.

Sound broadcasting covers three areas of Christian communication. First, worship. This may be broadcast direct from local churches on Sundays, and take the form of a morning service representing a particular tradition, a 'people's service' specially arranged for those who prefer less formal styles of worship, or a short programme of community hymn singing. The daily service, lasting fifteen minutes, is arranged and conducted by members of the BBC's own staff and is as firmly established in the pattern of broadcasting as are the news bulletins. All these programmes serve church members who, for various reasons, are unable to attend their local churches and are heard by many others who value a distant contact with worship, or who may feel drawn to listen at a particular moment of personal need, or who happen to have the radio switched on at the time and are attracted to give attention. As channels of Christian communication they are of limited usefulness, and it is clear that inadequately arranged services or tedious sermons may do a great deal of harm to the church's cause. Yet it is arguable (as I hope to demonstrate in the final chapter) that Christian worship can and should reflect accurately the heart of the Christian gospel.

The broadcasting of worship is supplemented by a daily diet of what may be described as 'inspirational' programmes – normally limited to five minutes and consisting of a talk or a story, to which prayers and music are added. Transmitted at breakfast time when radio broadcasting has its peak audiences, these programmes are heard (which is not the same as attended to) by millions of people. The quality varies enormously, from the brilliant to the banal depending on the skills of the broadcaster, and most producers will admit that, while they aim to achieve the highest standard, it is exceedingly difficult to locate a sufficient supply of religious communicators to meet the exacting demands of this type of programme. This is of course a reflection of the general weakness of the churches in communicating on the frontier of belief. Producers are also inhibited by the erroneous conviction of the BBC that devotion and controversy are incompatible, hence the absurd situation which developed in 1971 over the contributions of Colin Morris to the 'Thought for the Day' programmes, and led to his temporary withdrawal from them.

The third area covers a wide field of human concern, ranging from discussions with the Prime Minister about personal factors in politics to interviews with people suffering from terminal illness. Most recently, a series called 'Questions of Belief', in which a panel has attempted to answer the questions of local audiences, has evoked a good response and offered lively and informative programmes. The general standard of programmes presented in this area of religious broadcasting is well up to that of sound broadcasting in other spheres, and the production of a magazine-type programme on Sunday mornings (at present restricted to VHF channels) indicates that the staff of the religious broadcasting department of the BBC are as professionally competent as their colleagues in other departments. One member of the staff is also responsible for the production of programmes in which the intellectual demands on the listener are greater than normal and so find a place in the weekday output of radio three. Long and serious discussions with leading theologians and other churchmen are broadcast in this way and, though the total number in any year is not high, the standard of discussion is nearly always extremely good and these programmes make a valuable contribution to the general pattern of sound broadcasting. At the other extreme, a Sunday afternoon programme, 'Speak Easy', has brought a welcome and uncommon element of intelligent discussion into the radio one pop channel.

Besides the output of the religious broadcasting department, the BBC also employs a church affairs specialist in its news department to ensure adequate coverage of religious events and topical interviews with church leaders who are in the news. Again, the level of professional competence is just as high as that demanded of other specialist reporters and, although the amount of time devoted to religious affairs in news bulletins and news magazines is obviously controlled by the normal news factors, the output in any one week is considerable. So also is that of the schools broadcasting department, whose religious programmes achieve a uniformly high standard and are widely used, in conjunction with printed material, in the schools. The advent of local radio has also brought further opportunities for the broadcasting of opinion and news from the churches.

This sizeable operation of religious communication by means of the spoken word on radio costs the churches nothing; nor does it demand anything of them apart from a readiness to co-operate in the production of certain programmes. Yet no group of people serving the churches is subjected to more unkind or uninformed criticism than those responsible for this work. They would themselves be the first to admit that their programmes are not always perfect, and that some of them are disastrous failures (which is normal in every department of broadcasting), yet the fact remains that their skills in Christian communication are infinitely higher than those of the overwhelming majority of their critics. The churches would be well advised to provide the religious broadcasters with stronger support, better material on which to work, and show a greater readiness to learn from them the art of communication in a secular sphere.

What, then, of the traditional sermon, without which no act of worship is normally considered complete? Has this any place in the communication of the Christian faith in the present age? Many thoughtful people believe that the sermon is now outmoded and ought to be abandoned. They point out that standing a man in front of a passive audience, where he occupies a position 'six feet above contradiction', is discredited as a form of any kind of communication. It has largely disappeared from the classroom and the university. No one would dream of presenting a 'talking head' on a television screen for twenty minutes, unless the speaker was endowed with quite exceptional gifts of thought and language. Monologue, we are told, is no longer acceptable and the fact that many centuries of Christian preaching from pulpits has done no more than produce a largely ignorant laity seems to suggest that it has outlived its usefulness by a considerable span of years. There is no more damaging a charge to be laid against any public speaker than that he 'preached a sermon'. All of which seems to suggest that defence of preaching may require superhuman skill or, alternatively, an inhuman insensitivity.

Without claiming either attribute for myself, I remain to be convinced that there is no longer a place in the life of the church, and of the general community, for personal statements of conviction. Walk into Trafalgar Square or the market place of any large city on a Sunday afternoon and it is unusual not to find a man or woman, sometimes several men and women, expressing their convictions about something or other – Southern Africa, the Common Market, gay liberation, vivisection and so forth. Normally they have a crowd of supporters or of people who are interested to hear what they have to say. Just how effective they are in communicating their beliefs is an open question, yet the need for people to stand up and declare their convictions is surely important and far from redundant in the life of twentieth-century society. There are many parts of the world where one wishes that individuals had both the desire and the liberty to ventilate their opinions in this way.

If, therefore, it is in order for someone to give utterance from the plinth of Nelson's column or from the proverbial soap box, I am not easily persuaded that it is out of order for someone to speak from the pulpit of a church. At this point the question of personal conviction becomes crucial. The speakers in Trafalgar Square and other places of casual assembly are normally possessed by a quite passionate conviction about their subject. Hence their readiness to expose themselves to hostility or ridicule. And is this not precisely what one might expect of the Christian preacher? Which is not to suggest that he must rant and rave or throw his body about, but that he should always speak out of a deep inner conviction concerning the Christian faith and from an experience of Christ which is first, not second, hand.

The pulpit is not the place for propaganda or indoctrination. It is the place where an individual struggles to articulate, on behalf of himself or of the community of faith, something of the deep mystery of the Christian gospel as it impinges upon the lives of individuals and society in the contemporary world. The so-called 'teaching sermon' in which the the preacher simply offers some formal, and perhaps very carefully worked out, explanation of a particular Christian doctrine is therefore to be abhorred. This is not to say that the preacher must abandon theology, or that over a period of time he may not cover the main tenets of the Christian faith. It is to say that pulpit theology must be living theology in that it springs from the experience and dynamic conviction of the preacher and is directly related to the situations in which most human beings sooner or later find themselves at the personal and social levels.

Undoubtedly there is far too much preaching in most churches. The famous saying of Archbishop Launcelot Andrewes, 'He that preacheth twice on Sunday, prateth once', remains true for the overwhelming majority of those whom the church entrusts with the task of preaching. If a man or woman needs to reflect deeply on the meaning of life and the implications of Christian experience both for himself and for others, time is required. It is exceedingly difficult, if not actually impossible, to struggle to discover something of the truth when a clock or a diary is making other demands on one's time. Hence the unhelpful nature of so many sermons which have been compiled by a clergyman who, in the midst of many other tasks, is required to produce a hundred or more pulpit utterances every year. The idea – not much more than a hundred years old – that Christian communication is enhanced in direct proportion to the number of sermons preached, has proved to be disastrously wrong. It has driven the preacher to distraction and turned the proclamation of the gospel into a tiresome commonplace adjunct of worship.

With the exception of large town churches, serving different groups of people at various times of the day and adequately staffed, one sermon per Sunday ought to be quite adequate. The fact that there may be more than one priest or minister available is no reason for departing from this rule, since the preacher who has to produce only one sermon in a fortnight or an even longer interval is likely to be more helpful to those who hear him than the man who is required to make a weekly offering. Again, there is no reason why preaching should be confined to ordained ministers or accredited layman. The criterion for inviting a person to preach should not be his or her official status, but whether he or she has anything to say. Current regulations in most churches are designed to protect congregations from sermons which may not adequately reflect the doctrinal position of the body to which they belong. They have not been very successful, as any diligent listener to sermons will readily testify. But it is not the purpose of a sermon to propagate a 'party line' – orthodox or unorthodox; on the contrary, the sermon must be an attempt to express an experience or deeply held conviction. And there are members of every local congregation who have such experiences and convictions which they should be encouraged to share publicly with other members of the community to which they belong. In some instances they will need assistance with the presentation of what they wish to say, and in many cases a great deal of encouragement, but the introduction of more lay Christians into pulpits would transform the preaching in every church and help to make it the corporate activity it is meant to be. The preparation of sermons by groups, thus reflecting the beliefs and experiences of a number of Christians, would also assist in this direction.

A common complaint against preaching is that there is no opportunity to take issue with the preacher or even ask questions when points are in need of clarification. Dialogue sermons are an attempt to deal with this, and may on occasion be a much more effective form of communication, but experience suggests that they need most careful preparation and are far from being an easy way of avoiding the disciplined reflection required of the monologue preacher.

The answer to the complaint about the isolation of the preacher is to be found by recognizing that the sermon is only one small part of spoken communication. The undue emphasis which has been placed on the sermon – and provoked the current despair about its usefulness – has led to an almost total neglect of any other form of shared conversation in the churches. So great has been the confidence in the sermon that nothing else has been deemed necessary, apart from special groups for church membership training and so forth. The past twenty-five years has undoubtedly seen a degree of change here, with the development of house groups and other informal meetings for discussion, but present evidence suggests that the local churches where such groups form a regular and normal part of the life of the Christian community still constitute a fairly small minority, and that the proportion of any congregation involved in group work is even smaller.

Ample material is now available for consideration by Christian groups, ranging from Bible notes to cassette talks, but the real need is not for the study of 'injected' subjects or ideas. Much better for a group to pick up the theme of the last Sunday sermon they heard; even better for the group to develop the kind of relationships in which a free and frank interchange of conviction and experience is possible. Such an interchange need not be pietistic or introverted. It may well focus on some burning issue in the field of politics or concentrate on issues which are of special concern to people in particular vocational groups. The area of Christian concern knows no boundaries and whenever individuals are drawn into conversation about real human issues one may anticipate that a measure of communication and illumination will take place. So much has already been written about the vital importance of work at this level that it seems unnecessary to labour the point further. One can only note that the message has not yet been received by the church at large and that one of the clearest channels of communication has hardly begun to be used.

Another channel awaiting exploitation is that offered by the extra-mural departments of most British universities. Although they are secular institutions and unwilling to be used to promote the well-being of the churches, they recognize that religion is a valid field for human enquiry and, where there is a local demand, are nearly always prepared to provide courses of lectures and seminars at a level appropriate to university education. The Department of Adult Education at Manchester University has shown how much can be accomplished when resources and imagination are effectively linked. Extra-mural courses on aspects of contemporary theological thinking and on the relationship between religion and culture have attracted considerable numbers of students and been conducted on a high intellectual plane. The co-operation of local churches has been elicited in publicizing the courses, and there has been consultation over the securing of lecturers, but the facilities and finance have been provided by the university.

The Manchester experience, which has been confirmed in other universities, suggests quite clearly that the number of people, from inside and outside the churches, who are prepared to grapple with serious theological issues is increasing. Nor is the evidence confined to university centres. The Roman Catholic parish served by the Benedictine Priory of Christ the King at Cockfosters has for some years offered the locality a winter course in which theologians (sometimes of international repute) have discussed key theological themes with the laity. A regular attendance of 80–100 is achieved and an evening in 1971 when I was invited to present an introduction to the theology of Bonhoeffer, Bultmann and Tillich indicated beyond dispute that Cockfosters is now producing a significant number of lay theologians. Rarely have I attended a more encouraging meeting.

Since Cockfosters is a highly privileged London suburb, in which the number of people who have had some form of higher education is well above national average, one is not entitled to conclude that every local church could provide similar fare for its people. In any case, there would not be sufficient teaching resources to go round. But in towns and other centres of population it should be possible to mount courses for those who are willing and able to consume a fair amount of intellectual meat, and unless the churches recognize that the current growth in higher education is now making new demands on those responsible for Christian communication, the outlook for the churches and for the Christian faith itself is bound to be bleak.

Nowhere is this more plain to see than in the colleges of education. The question of the future of religious education in schools lies outside the scope of this book, but it is impossible to consider the subject of Christian communication without taking notice of the massive investment which the British churches (in particular the Church of England) have in the training of teachers. Granted that attempts at indoctrination are objectionable on both theological and educational grounds, and also that religious education is not to be conceived in terms of certain periods of religious instruction provided for in school timetables, what have the church's colleges of education to offer that cannot be obtained elsewhere? Is there any longer a case for the churches to deploy any part of their diminishing resources in this field?

The answer must surely be that the churches should only remain in the sphere of teacher training if they have something quite distinctive to offer. Having entered the sphere in a pioneering role in the nineteenth century, the question now is whether the church colleges of education can continue to pioneer. One is entitled to hope that they can. The most fundamental human need at the present time is the ability to see life whole; to discover how the many pieces of knowledge and experience may be brought together to form a complete and harmonious picture, thus enabling men and women to live their lives to the full. There is evidence that religious insight and experience have a significant part to play in securing for individuals, as well as for society as a whole, growth towards unity and harmony. Hence the importance of institutions in which Christians are encouraged to pursue the quest for wholeness in their own lives and to translate this into terms which may be shared with those who attend the nation's schools. Some of those attending church colleges of education will, it may be anticipated, continue to specialize in particular aspects of academic theology – scripture, church history, ethics, etc. – but of infinitely greater importance is the need for the colleges to become laboratories of wholeness in which the essential unity of human life is recognized and its implications worked out in terms of the society which a school exists to serve. It is doubtful whether such an approach can be effectively carried out with a concentration of people whose sights are set on teaching in schools. The incorporation into the colleges of people who are training for ordination, social and community work, and medicine would be an important factor in creating the right conditions for research. Such an institution would have much to offer in our increasingly fragmented society and become an important channel of Christian communication.

Having considered a number of actual and potential channels of communication open to those who wish to share their Christian insights and experience with others by means of the spoken word, it is now necessary to turn to a fundamental question about the point from which such a sharing should normally begin. For the greater part of Christian history – though not, it should be noted, for every part – the starting point of Christian communication has been the declaration of 'received' Christian truth. The communicator has read or expounded a passage from the Bible, or called attention to a credal statement or some other dogmatic formulation. He has then attempted to relate this to some other aspect of truth or experience in an attempt to reach a synthesis which his listener would find compelling. The best communicators have provided a reasoned basis for their Christian stance, but their starting point has always been revelation or tradition.

This remains true for the overwhelming majority of those who are concerned with Christian communication at the present time. The preacher nearly always begins his discourse with an exposition of scripture and moves from this to an application of the discerned truth to the lives of those who make up his congregation. An academic theologian invariably teaches or writes in terms of elucidating or applying a biblical or dogmatic statement. It was particularly noticeable at the meeting of the Faith and Order Commission of the World Council of Churches held at Louvain in the summer of 1971 to consider 'The Unity of the Church and the Unity of Mankind' that all but a handful of the 200 distinguished theologians present were committed to beginning their approach to the subject from the point of faith.

Yet it is becoming increasingly clear that there is little scope for illumination or communication by this means. Neither the scriptural statement nor the dogmatic formulation is self-evidently true. In both cases certain presuppositions call for most careful scrutiny and evaluation. Nor is it possible to discover the truth of the statements in isolation from other aspects of truth or the experience of those to whom they are addressed.

The need, then, is for the Christian to sit alongside those who are concerned with the various important elements in human life – the physician, the sociologist, the scientist, the artist, the psychologist, the politician – and when he has discovered from them what they have learned about the human condition, and what they have to contribute to man's ultimate well-being, he may be in a position to suggest ways in which Christian faith can be an integrating and enhancing element in the process.

I have especially in mind here the professional theologian, whose work in the isolation of the study and library has brought the communication of the Christian faith almost to a complete stop. There is now a quite desperate need for theological research to be carried out in a multi-disciplinary setting. But what is true of the academic level is equally true of every other level of Christian sharing. The preacher who is bold enough to share his convictions with others from a church pulpit must take the trouble to listen to those to whom he speaks and to discover what influences are at work in their lives. His own understanding of the nature of truth is likely to be increased in the process and when he ventilates his own beliefs he is more likely to be able to express them in terms which are meaningful to those who listen to him. Needless to say, the same is true of other forms of Christian communication, whether this takes place in groups or in private conversation.

My plea is for Christians to show a greater readiness to listen and to learn. Effective channels of communication demand the possibility of two-way traffic. Pontificating, dogmatizing and shouting have never been very effective means of sharing either insight or experience. They are completely outmoded in the present stage of human development and, while due allowance has to be made for the natural enthusiasm of those who are suddenly possessed by what is for them a new revelation, the emphasis today must be on openness and humility.

The pontificator will immediately protest that this approach involves a betrayal of responsibility towards those who are looking for the security offered by disclosures of revealed truth and is, in any case, certain to lead to a dilution of the gospel. But such protests must not be allowed to divert those who are concerned with Christian communication from the right way forward. That there are, and always have been, individuals seeking security through the acceptance of what appears to be infallible truth cannot be doubted. But it is no part of the church's task to minister to this need. On the contrary, if the church is to assist men and women towards maturity and fulness of life it must take great pains to ensure that their security is based on qualities of love and faith and trust and not on the bogus security offered by a dogmatic statement, even though this statement has become the truth for many who have accepted it. Hence the need for the Christian communicator to avoid the temptation to make easy gains through the exploitation of human weakness and inadequacy which may be traced to psychological roots.

Moreover, the readiness to listen to and learn from those whose approach to the truth is along paths other than those provided by Christian doctrine and experience, does not imply any readiness to abandon firmly held convictions. Those few theologians and pastors who have shown openness at this level have manifestly been motivated by a deep and burning desire to share their experience of Christ with other people. It is far easier to adopt a dogmatic 'take it or leave it' approach which places the responsibility for non-communication solely upon the shoulders of those who cannot receive what is offered. Bishop John Robinson would have found life far more congenial had he followed the example of the rest of his episcopal colleagues and devoted his ministry in Southwark to the patient exposition of traditional doctrine. But his deep concern for the people of South London, whom he perceived to be incapable of receiving such doctrine, led him to grapple with a form of Christian expression in the hope that the heart of the gospel might be exposed and recognized. *Honest to God* was in no sense a sell-out to atheistic humanism. The real betrayal of the gospel is being perpetrated by those who are concealing it from twentieth-century man by over-protection of the verbal and philosophical forms which earlier generations adopted for the purpose of communication in their own time.

Looking back over the 1960s, when the radical explosion occurred in Britain, it is now apparent that those who lit the fuses did not take sufficient care to make plain their motivation. It was too easy for those who opposed the new theological movement to accuse its leaders of betrayal and heresy, thus driving radicals on to the defensive. A better approach would have been to emphasize the deep and genuine concern felt for those who were not even in a position to give the Christian faith serious consideration, because of its cultural accretions, and to have exposed the inadequacy of the utterances of church leaders, preachers and teachers at every level of the nation's life. Those required to appear before the bar of judgment are not the communicators seeking new ways of expressing their Christian convictions, but those who persist in sheltering under the threadbare umbrella of traditional doctrines.

This remains true at the beginning of the 1970s. It is not easy for Christians to lend support to what appears to be a negative approach, yet considerable demolition work is frequently required before new edifices can be erected, and though few people believe the present time to be ripe for major theological reconstruction, the time for a serious and penetrating critique of much that passes for Christian orthodoxy is long overdue.

Willingness to listen to those working in other fields of human experience, and readiness to modify one's own position in the light of new information or experience is a sign, not of betrayal or cowardice, but of a deep trust in both the depth and the breadth of God's creative activity in the world. It indicates a belief that divine light may be reflected as clearly through the mirror of the scientist as through the mirror of the New Testament scholar. It indicates a depth of conviction and commitment which is prepared to run the risks of abandoning a previously held belief in order to come within reach of a new revelation or a more authentic experience. There is no element of diminution here. On the contrary, there is a vision of a God who is in no way dependent upon limited human skill and insight, and who is ready to share his light and love with the whole of humanity.

This open and other-ended approach to the study and communication of Christian truth has been discussed here with special reference to the spoken word. But it applies to all forms of communication as those who are working on the frontiers of faith and doubt are well aware. Risks are involved and mistakes are not impossible among the adventurous. There is no evidence to suggest that those who approach communication from this direction will be successful, in the sense of making more recruits for the churches. But there is ample evidence that they are able to become involved in a real sharing of insight and experience, and that their contribution to man's search for meaning and purpose is welcomed and appreciated. This must be regarded as a significant breakthrough, pointing the way forward.

# 6     The Visual Word

If this book had been written in 1922 and not in 1972 it would certainly have been necessary to occupy a lot of space arguing the importance of the eye as a crucially important gateway to communication. Chapters would have been devoted to the physical connection between the eye and the brain, to the deep impression made in the mind by sight of a mountain or a picture or a diagram. An attempt would have been made to show that the presentation of a piece of information or the relating of an experience was, for a great many people, best accomplished through something visual.

It is, one presumes and hopes, no longer necessary to argue this case. The experience of the classroom, the magazine, the advertisement hoarding and the television screen has proved the point. Few people would venture into the field of communication at any level without some form of visual aid and even those journals designed for an intellectual readership now find it necessary, or at least desirable, to make some 'concessions' to the eye through the use of drawings and photographs.

The question for the churches in Britain is why, in the light of the experience of the past fifty years, they make so little use of visual means of communication? In spite of a few forays into visual territory, the main thrust of the church's work of communication remains verbal. It is still assumed that if something is said with sufficient conviction, subtlety or frequency it will sooner or later register in the minds of those who hear it. Conservatism undoubtedly explains some of the church's reluctance to accept the visual as a major channel of communication. It is sometimes pointed out that visual aids are costly and that skill in visual presentation is rare and not easily acquired. All of which suggests that the churches have still not got the message. The fact that their leadership is drawn from those intellectual elites which are (according to conventional wisdom) less dependent upon visual presentation means that little emphasis is placed upon this aspect of communication and so the necessary resources are not available for development in this direction. Religious books containing photographs or drawings are confined to ecclesiastical biographies, in which sight of the subject is considered important; geographies of the Holy Land, where readers are given proof that places like Nazareth and Jerusalem actually exist; and children's books, in which a certain concession to the eye is recognized but rarely expressed in other than misleading terms. The use of visual material in the training of clergy and ministers is virtually unknown, much less training clergy and ministers in the use of such material. Hence the fact that in local churches visual material, outside Sunday schools and the like, is confined to the occasional showing of a film of doubtful quality, when the only certainty is that the opening sequence will appear upside down and the sound track break down at least three times during the first half hour of the programme.

In these circumstances it is necessary to look first, and mainly, at the presentation of religious insight and experience as it is portrayed by means of television. The circumstances in which religion finds any place in the television world are not different from those which give it a place in sound broadcasting. Again it must be emphasized that neither the British Broadcasting Corporation nor the Independent Television Authority see themselves as handmaids of the churches. It is not their function to assist in recruitment to church membership or even to contribute to the making, or keeping, of Britain Christian. Their task is to inform, educate and entertain and religion will only find a place on broadcasting schedules for as long as those responsible for broadcasting believe it to be important enough to a significant number of viewers and listeners to justify the use of expensive resources.

The current output of BBC television in the religious field consists of a Sunday morning act of worship, normally devised specially for television production, and a 'serious' forty-minute programme, consisting of discussions, features and documentaries, broadcast during the early part of Sunday evening and followed by a thirty-minute programme of hymn singing from a local church. From time to time programmes of a definable religious character are broadcast on weekdays but their appearances are infrequent, and religion has little place in the BBC's second channel. A Director of Religious Television is employed, under the Head of Religious Broadcasting, and is assisted by a team of five producers.

Independent Television follows a somewhat similar pattern, although the structure of its organization is much more complicated. A service broadcast live from a local church occupies an hour on Sunday morning and attempts to cover the denominational and geographical spread of the mainstream churches. 6.15 p.m. is the appointed hour for approximately forty-five minutes of 'serious' programming and this is followed by half an hour of 'popular' hymn singing. In many parts of Britain, depending upon the policy of the regional companies, the day's broadcasting concludes with a five-minute programme consisting of varied fare; sometimes a local clergyman offering an uplifting homily, sometimes an interview, occasionally music and prayer It is rare for a programme produced by the religious departments of any of the companies to be transmitted during peak viewing hours on weekdays.

The concentration of religious broadcasting in the early part of Sunday evening has been determined by government policy which decreed, on the resumption of television at the end of World War II, that there should be no television broadcasting between 6.15 p.m. and 7.25 p.m. except for programmes of a religious character, outside broadcasts of special events and Welsh language programmes. This applied to every day of the week and was designed to protect family life. When 'toddlers' hour' was eventually abolished the churches persuaded the government to retain its ruling in respect of Sunday; this time for the protection of church services. During the past five years there has been much debate about the propriety and value of this so-called 'closed period'. Those approaching the subject from the secular angle have questioned whether religion should be protected in this way. Some of those deeply concerned about religious broadcasting have suggested that protection has bred complacency about programme standards.

The answer to those who believe that the 'closed period' provides religion with specially favoured treatment is not too difficult to find. Examination of the *Radio Times* and the *TV Times* indicates that programme scheduling is not an unplanned operation. The BBC and the ITA are aware of the need to maintain some sort of balance in their output and also to take account of the rhythms and patterns which form part of the lives of viewers. So, while drama enjoys no official protection and might, theoretically, disappear from the television screen altogether, no one believes that plays will ever occupy less than several hours of viewing time every week. Again, there is no compulsion to televise sporting events but a major upheaval would be required to secure the removal of the Saturday afternoon sports programmes. All channels are required to broadcast news bulletins and could present these at whatever hours suited their convenience, but there would be a public outcry if they departed from the 'sacred' hours of 6 p.m., 9 p.m. and 10 p.m., and in fact the familiar faces of the newscasters are rarely seen at any other times. Many elements in television broadcasting are therefore afforded an unofficial protection which, in practice, is not very different from religion's closed period.

There are, of course, some Christians who believe that religion is so important to the health of individuals and of the nation that it *ought* to receive specially favoured treatment in the television world and that it *ought* to be protected against any other pressures which might dislodge it from its established place in the present pattern of broadcasting. But even among those who cannot accept this propagandist or paternalistic approach to Christian communication there has been a certain nervousness about supporting any proposal for the abolition of the closed period. This nervousness is based on a fundamental mistrust of those responsible for broadcasting in Britain. While it is acknowledged that religion ought to be able to stand on its own feet, and that those concerned with Christian communication should be ready to compete with other producers for a share in the amount of television time available, there is little confidence that the resources would be made available for religious producers to enter into effective competition.

All television production is costly in terms of equipment and personnel. While it is true that some programmes of a very high quality have been produced on a shoe-string and that some extremely expensive productions have been dismal failures, it remains true that money determines to a very large extent the kind of programmes we see in any field of television broadcasting. This is not simply a matter of the amount of money made available to a producer for the translation of an idea into reality, important though this certainly is. It also concerns the number of creative minds who are employed in a particular department. Of all the mass media, none is more demanding on its personnel than is television. The challenge to produce ideas which can be translated into visual form and thus communicated to millions of people who are looking at a small box in their homes is immensely stimulating to certain people, but always exhausting. The rise and fall of personalities is a normal part of life in the television world. In no other sphere are individuals so easily 'burned out' and regarded as either expendable or passengers. The maintenance of a staff which is adequate in terms of size and ability is therefore quite crucial to the maintenance of broadcasting standards. Some doubt exists as to whether the BBC or the Independent companies are prepared to meet this requirement in terms of religious television; hence the desire of a number of people, who would otherwise favour a more 'open' situation, to retain a closed period in order that at least some religious programmes should be broadcast and some personnel employed for the purpose. Another factor entering into the discussion concerns the times at which programmes are transmitted. A fear exists that, even if religion continues to find a place in television, it might be relegated to a time of the day when viewing audiences are, for sociological reasons, at their lowest. The 'closed period' has at least guaranteed a certain amount of peak viewing time on one evening of the week. Again, mistrust is an important factor in the discussion.

There are, it must be frankly admitted, good reasons for this mistrust. And here it is necessary to distinguish rather carefully between the dynamics of the BBC and the Independent companies. The distinction applies across the entire field of television and is not peculiar to religious broadcasting. It produces two different problems.

As a public corporation which receives its income from licence fees, and is therefore exempt from most commercial pressures, the BBC enjoys a degree of financial freedom which is entirely absent from the realm of commercial television. But the price it pays for this freedom is bureaucracy. Broadcasting House functions in much the same way as a government ministry, with its hierarchy, protocol, carefully formulated procedures and caution. Although the staff are not always happy, they are for the most part secure and, once appointed, may anticipate continuous employment until the day they draw their pensions. Such an organization, while encouraging a high sense of responsibility and providing substantial resources for programme production, does not produce an atmosphere in which true creativity easily flourishes. Furthermore, the 'civil service' type terms of employment often lead to the retention of staff beyond the time when their creativity is exhausted. Religious television has suffered considerably because of this, and the problem has been exacerbated by the fact that it has not proved possible to transfer its excellent specialist producers to other departments where they might take on a new lease of life. This is a delicate matter. It is extremely undesirable that men and women should be treated as expendable and simply cast aside when they can no longer meet the demands of an organization. On the other hand, the maintenance of creativity is crucial to the development of television and this demands a staff of adequate size and mobility. There are signs that the BBC is now becoming more sensitive to this problem in religious broadcasting by employing staff who are able to be moved from the religious department to other departments and by offering only fairly short-term contracts to clergymen who wish to specialize in the field but may return to work in their churches when they have made a useful contribution. Unfortunately, the fruits of this policy are still somewhat meagre.

The position in the Independent television companies is quite different. Here money is the primary consideration. This should surprise no one, since the basis on which commercial television came into existence was frankly commercial and, though the financial benefits to shareholders are no longer as substantial as in the early days when Lord Thomson of Fleet found that his television franchise was the equivalent of 'a licence to print money', the accountants are undoubtedly more important than the programme controllers and producers. In effect, this means that money is available for lavish programmes designed to command large audiences at peak-viewing times, and therefore able to attract substantial advertising revenue, but tends to be in short supply for programmes of minority interest unless questions of prestige are involved. Such a situation undoubtedly stimulates creativity of a certain kind, and has attracted some of the most able producers and performers, but it obviously has an inhibiting effect upon those who wish to experiment or cater for relatively small numbers of viewers, i.e. under five million. The turn-over in staff is, as one might expect, very considerable. Contracts are short and quickly terminated once an individual has outlived his usefulness to a company.

Needless to say, religion tends to figure well down the table of commercial priorities and the resources available for religious programmes are small. At the beginning of 1972 London Weekend Television was the only company of the fifteen employing any full-time staff (two) exclusively on religious programmes. The rest, some of whose output is small, since they find it more economical to purchase programmes from major companies, use producers who are involved in current affairs, drama or educational programmes. The manpower position is not, however, quite as bleak as it first appears, for each company has a group of advisers (usually three, drawn from the mainstream Christian traditions) who are involved in the consideration of ideas, selection of performers and, sometimes, in the actual production of

92

programmes. The degree of involvement varies from company to company, and in some instances is both substantial and creative, but it is obvious that part-time advisers can never be a substitute for full-time professional staff. Neither can the ingenuity of producers, whose interests probably lie in some other field, always overcome the stringent budgetary arrangements which dominate the making of almost every religious programme.

These, then, are the main sources of anxiety about the ending of the 'closed period'. If such formidable difficulties have to be faced 'in the green', what obstacles might have to be overcome 'in the dry'? But while churchmen and others were immersed in a protracted debate about the future of the 'closed period', the Minister of Posts and Communications swept it away in January 1972 in the course of a fiat directing that all restriction on television should be removed. Whether the Minister was aware of what he was doing in the sphere of religious television when he issued his directive is far from clear. Certainly he did not consult anyone who might have had views on the subject, for example, the Central Religious Advisory Committee, though he did obtain assurances from the broadcasting authorities that they would not change the present balance of their programme schedules, in which religion has a recognized place. Legally, there is no longer a 'closed period', but it seems likely that in the short term the present pattern of religious television will remain the same, by agreement between the BBC and the ITA, neither of which bodies is yet ready to enter into public controversy or cut-throat competition in the sphere of religion. In the long term, however, certain changes seem inevitable. On the negative side, religious programmes may be relegated to unpopular hours of the day or night when only devotees or desperate viewers will switch on their sets. Positively, it may prove possible for high-quality religious programmes to find a place in mid-week peak viewing periods. It is impossible to forecast in which direction either the BBC or the ITA will move, though it would be reasonable to suppose that their courses might be set by the underlying bases on which they already function.

Unfortunately, the existence of the 'closed period' for so

many years has inhibited any sustained and serious discussion about the nature of religious television and the constituents of a 'religious' programme. The degree of confusion which now exists at this point was amply demonstrated by three programmes presented on the Independent network during the 'closed period' on Sunday, 23 January 1972. From 6.15–6.30 p.m. Anglia Television contributed a profile of *A Twentieth-Century Bishop*. This was a misleading title, for while the recently-appointed Bishop of Norwich (who was the subject of the programme) undoubtedly lives in the twentieth century, the greater part of his thought and action is derived from the reign of Queen Victoria. The combination of athleticism, bonhomie and 'Come to Jesus' piety was therefore depressing for any sensitive Christian viewer and extremely off-putting to others who might have been interested in what a modern bishop does with his time or who just chanced to keep his set switched on after the six o'clock news. If the evangelical mind ever became influential in religious television, viewers would doubtless be subjected to a great deal of material of this kind. Fortunately, it is far too crude to qualify for more than an occasional outing.

The Bishop of Norwich was followed by *Adam Smith*, a fictitious Church of Scotland minister making his first appearance in a new series of programmes produced by Granada Television. This was a bold and imaginative attempt to break new ground in religious television by means of a drama serial based on the human stresses experienced by a fairly typical cleric whose wife met an early death and the course of whose work was changed in consequence. Good acting, a script written by someone well acquainted with the human condition, an unusually ample production budget and a firm determination not to offer an 'answer' or point a 'moral' resulted in thirty minutes of first class television. For many viewers, *Adam Smith* provided a new experience of religious television and, within a few weeks, it had an audience of fourteen million and the promise of a long run.

Any encouragement or enlightenment thus experienced was quickly neutralized by the inevitable arrival at 7 p.m. of *Stars on Sunday*. Produced by Yorkshire Television, this regular Sunday evening programme offered its normal sequence of hymns and Bible readings, sung and read by famous personalities operating in a typical show-biz atmosphere and setting. A quite deliberate emphasis on sentiment, nostalgia and escapism results in a massive audience of seventeen million viewers and places the programme among the most popular broadcasts in Britain. The only difficulty now is whether the programme can properly be described as 'religious'. Of those who believe that *Stars on Sunday* is not religious, the most charitable would classify it as entertainment while the rest would classify it as a unique programme of unbridled cynicism. It is no secret that this programme has caused considerable disquiet among those who are concerned for the future of religious television, yet it may in the end be the only programme of an allegedly religious content to retain a place in early Sunday evening broadcasting. The massive ratings achieved by *Stars on Sunday* are valuable to the programme companies not only for the twenty-five minutes it occupies the screen but also for its effects on the viewing figures for the remainder of the evening. There is evidence that those who turn to a particular channel at 7 p.m. remain on the same channel until bedtime – a fact which cannot be overlooked by those who wish to obtain the highest possible rates for advertising spots.

It is impossible to move into the world of broadcasting without becoming acutely aware of the extent to which viewer ratings influence policy. That this should be so is not in itself discreditable. If a producer or performer believes in the worth of what he is doing, it is natural that he should wish as many people as possible to see the result. And it is extremely important that the wishes of viewers should be taken into account when programme schedules are planned. Translated into the sphere of religious broadcasting, it is hardly wrong for a communicator to desire a large audience, nor is it a sin to try to meet the expressed needs of those who switch on their sets. But a serious concern about ratings is only legitimate when those responsible for broadcasting are strong enough to resist enslavement by ratings and are therefore prepared to produce programmes which will not necessarily attract wide audiences.

Given the present climate of opinion in Britain, it is reasonable to suppose that programmes labelled 'religious' will naturally fall into this category. In my view, better programmes would result from clearer recognition of this fact and from the deliberate exploitation of the freedom which such recognition would provide. The dangers of the alternative approach are clearly exemplified by the most recent policy of the BBC's religious broadcasting department. In an attempt to attract more viewers, the BBC decided in 1970 to employ Mr Malcolm Muggeridge as the presenter of a series of discussion programmes during the Sunday 'closed period'. Mr Muggeridge is an accomplished broadcaster, with a remarkable command of the English language and so well known that he has become a household name. For the greater part of his life he was an outspoken opponent of the Christian faith and a staunch critic of the church, but his later years have seen a gradual conversion to a form of religious belief which includes certain Christian elements tinged with Manichaeism. St Augustine and Pascal have played a part in his conversion. The fact that Mr Muggeridge already had a fairly considerable band of admirers in the country seemed a good enough reason for providing him with a key position in religious broadcasting; the expectation being that a significant number of viewers would be prepared to tune in to a religious programme in order to hear Mr Muggeridge. The result of this thinking was the domination by Mr Muggeridge of BBC religious television for the next two years. The details of the programme were varied slightly – the size and composition of the discussion group being changed from time to time – but the basic formula remained the same: Mr Muggeridge in the role of prima donna, the panel providing a corps de ballet. In consequence, Mr Muggeridge became (and may still be) the chief spokesman for the Christian faith on BBC television and this, not because anyone believed his insights to be particularly valuable or even Christian, but because he had the ability to attract an audience. It is hard to conceive of a more disastrous approach to religious television than this.

If, however, it proves possible to be less concerned about high ratings, producers may then be able to give rather more serious consideration to the question of whom the religious programmes are intended to serve, a question which seems fundamental to any approach to communication and which might with profit have been faced some time ago. Much of the present confusion about aims, and many of the inferior programmes presented, can be traced to the failure to deal with this question. If, for example, the programmes are directed towards people who already have a Christian commitment and may belong to a church, they will obviously have a different content from programmes directed towards viewers who are interested outsiders. Again, if the aim is to communicate with children the programme content will be different from that offered to elderly people who are seeking comfort and assurance. This seems so obvious as not to require mentioning, yet it is plain for all to see that the overwhelming majority of religious programmes are not designed for anyone in particular but simply for the great admass who may be persuaded to tune in by the attraction of a recognizable name or an interesting subject.

It is when the aim of the producer is to attract and hold the attention of the interested outsider that the major question is raised about the nature of a religious programme. Occasionally, a programme about some aspect of the church's life will serve the purpose since the church is still a national institution of considerable size and revelations concerning its internal dynamics may arouse a certain curious interest. Programmes about the Vatican or the Church of England or the Salvation Army are still to be seen in popular secular programmes like *Panorama*. But these cannot be offered too frequently and the normal approach to the outsider must be oblique or parabolic.

At this point certain ethical issues have to be faced. If the purpose of religious television is to win converts to the Christian faith, the use of oblique or parabolic methods is either dishonest or manipulative – or both. Here we are on the treacherous territory where the mass media is used for purposes of propaganda. The fact that the propaganda is thought to be good and beneficial is immaterial; all propagandists begin from this premise. An oblique approach can only be justified when based on a conviction that in the final resort religious television is concerned not with making the viewer a Christian but with helping him to become a more mature human being by inviting him to reflect on some of the fundamental elements which belong to his humanity. This is not to suggest that religious programmes can simply be a repetition of current affairs material, dominated by political, social and economic problems. On the contrary, while religious programmes cannot ignore the fact that man does live by bread, they must also remind viewers than man does not live by bread alone. Such a statement is not to be classified as religious propaganda because it is in fact a statement about the human condition which every viewer knows to be true. Programmes which provoke reflection on the factors in human relations, the nature of evil, the power of love, the dilemma of choice in complex situations, the significance of death, the meaning of commitment, the agonies of loyalty (to mention just a few subjects) may therefore be classified as religious. Each is capable of providing insight into the character of that kingdom where love, joy, peace, righteousness and freedom reign.

Once this is recognized the field of religious television is seen to be very much wider than that occupied by the producers of 'religious programmes'. Perhaps the best religious programmes yet produced were seen in Kenneth Clarke's magnificent series on *Civilization*. Many of the best television plays have a high religious content in that they convey something of the agony and the ecstasy experienced by the human spirit. Programmes of music and dancing can again evoke in the viewer aspirations and feelings and insights which are essentially religious. Such programmes are devised without the assistance of theologians or religious producers, and are none the worse for that, but a strong case can be advanced for having some members of religious broadcasting staffs detached from their own department and allowed to roam at will in other spheres where their contribution to the planning of secular programmes would be welcomed. Needless to say, such men or women would have to win their way by a recognizable combination of ability and integrity, but owning these qualities they might well find freedom to make a contribution in a medium whose demand for ideas and insights is insatiable.

Here one is bound to record disappointment with the achievements of the Churches Television Centre. Heavily subsidized by the late Lord Rank, the millionaire Methodist, this centre has largely failed because its aims were from the outset defective. The emphasis at Bushey is focused far too heavily on the techniques of production. The setting up of a fully equipped studio, at colossal expense, has enabled the staff to introduce a large number of clergymen and theological students to the conditions produced by lighting, cameras and microphones. Courses have challenged parish ministers with problems involved in communication which they had not previously considered. A number of films have been made for showing in church halls and other establishments. But the influence upon religious television as it appears through the channels of public broadcasting in Britain has been negligible. Of the thousands of people who have passed through the centre, only a handful have ever appeared with any frequency on the television screen, and this for the simple reason that neither the BBC nor the Independent companies recruit their broadcasters from a 'trained pool' awaiting employment. Those who appear on television do so because they have a natural gift for communication through this particular medium or have some special contribution to make to a particular programme. People in either category will obviously improve with experience but 'training' is not the means of entry into this highly competitive and demanding world.

Of far greater value would be a centre with only a modest amount of equipment – sufficient to show films of actual programmes – and a strong emphasis on research and reflection. The official ending of the 'closed period' and the possibility of religion having to tread a totally new path in the world of television, finds the British churches without any coherent view of the nature of religious television or any concept of how to exert a creative influence on the most powerful communications medium of the present time. A centre which had concentrated on bringing together the best minds from the fields of theology and communication at intervals over a long period might by now have had something extremely valuable to show for its efforts. Furthermore, it would have provided a useful seedbed for ideas. It cannot be emphasized too strongly that television's appetite for ideas is insatiable. Those who are aware of the medium's possibilities and limitations may be sure that their ideas for programmes will always receive serious consideration. A large proportion – probably the majority – of ideas submitted are rejected, for many different reasons. But a research centre, in close touch with work being carried out in other parts of the world and sensitive to the essentially broad character of religious television, might well have exercised a considerable, even if hidden, influence on television in Britain during the past decade.

Since the greater part of this chapter has been devoted to television, it is necessary, before moving on to other fields of visual communication, to mention two factors which are frequently overlooked or misunderstood. The first of these concerns the youthfulness of the medium. Producers of religious programmes are subjected to a great deal of criticism, especially from within the churches. There is ample scope for criticism and no useful purpose is served by offering bouquets when brickbats are called for. Yet we are still in the very early days of television and much remains to be learned about the medium and the most effective means of production. Those responsible for religious programmes are faced with the most difficult task of all, since their subject often obstinately refuses to be translated into tele-visual terms, and much of the criticism levelled against them would be more helpful and have stronger force if it sprang from an understanding of what is involved in working with this highly complex and sensitive medium.

The second factor concerns the actual influence of television on individuals and on society. This is nearly always over-estimated. The fact that millions of people see a particular programme and that the skilled use of a visual medium offers many special opportunities easily leads to the conclusion that television has an almost hypnotic effort upon human attitudes and behaviour. There is, fortunately, little evidence that this is the case. On the contrary, viewers remain remarkably unaffected by the virtues and vices they see portrayed on the screen. As the purveyor of certain kinds of information television is often very effective and in particular situations, of which the Pakistani war of 1971 is perhaps the most notable example, it can heighten the viewers' awareness of what is taking place. But few people remember more than a tiny part of what they have seen and experienced by means of television. So, while the general effect of television on the social and cultural life of Britain has been very considerable, and while the importance of religious television is very great, the churches should not suppose that it provides *the* answer to their communications problem. On the whole, it would be far safer to assume that its contribution is fairly small.

Since drama has grown from religious origins, it is hardly surprising that plays are sometimes a most powerful channel for the communication of religious truth. The involvement of the individuals who make up the audience in the action of a play, by means of visual techniques and human actors, can lead to the communicating of an experience or an idea or a question in a form which is, for some, virtually irresistible. One might anticipate, therefore, that the church would have a quite heavy investment in contemporary drama, recognizing it to be an indispensable tool in the communication of the gospel. In fact, apart from the valiant work of the Religious Drama Society, the church is hardly in touch with the world of drama, much less deeply involved in it. This is not to say that plays are never seen in churches. Christmas inevitably brings out the children in blankets and towels to portray incidents from the nativity of Christ. Occasionally there are productions of *Murder in the Cathedral* or more avant garde offerings like *Christ in the Concrete City*. But all these belong to the outer fringes of the church's communication work and, while the efforts of the amateur actors are praiseworthy, the effectiveness of the productions is, to say the least, questionable.

Which is not to say that there is a shortage of religious drama. On the contrary, a great deal in the contemporary theatre is highly religious in character, if by 'religious' we mean concern for the ultimate questions about man and his destiny. The plays of Brecht, Tennessee Williams, Ionesco, Camus and Beckett are essentially theological in content, even though some of their authors are avowedly atheist. Students for the ordained ministry would learn far more about the nature of God and man, and be much better equipped for their work in local communities, if they were compelled to attend the theatre once a week instead of the lectures of a professor. Harvey Cox has argued convincingly for the religious character of the notorious musical *Hair*, and, as in the case of the parables of Jesus, there is a great deal of insight and nourishment to be gained in the theatre by those who have ears to hear and eyes to see.

Fortunately, the offerings of the dramatist do not depend upon the patronage of the church and it is arguable that, given the present condition of the church, it may be an advantage for the church to be far removed from this particular field of communication. Certainly any attempt to introduce an evangelical note into the proceedings would be disastrous, and it would not of course be tolerated, or even understood, by the majority of the most gifted playwrights of our time. Even so, it is disturbing that some of the best Christian theologians have not found it possible to enter into dialogue with their opposite numbers in the theatre. The life-style of a playwright or an actor may be somewhat different from that of a professional theologian, but each is essentially a serious man investigating, often at the cost of intense personal anguish, crucial questions about human nature and reality. If a Christian theologian is prepared to concede that not even the gospel presents him with ready made answers to all, or even any, of these questions, there opens up the possibility of dialogue and sharing of insight.

The benefits of such a sharing would be immeasurable for all concerned. The theologian would be constantly challenged by those who are tackling the same issues as himself but from a different – some would assert more realistic – angle. On the other hand, the playwright would benefit from contact with men whose lives are devoted to reflecting upon life's ultimate questions in a disciplined way and with reference to the experience and insights of the past. There is always a risk that the contemporary theatre will become remote from contemporary life as its chief artists are captured by the fascination of experiment. Once again, one is confronted by a familiar, and disturbing problem: the acute shortage of Christians who have the skill and sensitivity to walk with ease along the frontier between faith and doubt. In the present climate in Britain those who can do this are still able to exercise a remarkably creative role. The amount of avowed atheism and anti-clericalism is negligible. Men and women are valued, not for the ideology they embrace, but for the insights they can bring to bear upon matters of common concern. Obviously, the 'hot gospellers' are completely out of their depth in situations of this kind, and had better stay within their churches, but any reflective Christian who is ready to listen and to share can find a welcome in the world of the theatre, and indeed in the sphere of the arts as a whole.

It would be unreasonable to expect that large numbers of such Christians might emerge overnight. And it had better be understood that bodies like the Actors' Church Union provide neither starting point nor guide. But there is a desperate need for an initiative to be taken in the field of drama and also in the visual arts field where there is a great deal of religious insight being expressed but little contact with those who have been inspired by the Christian revelation. The late Bishop George Bell of Chichester saw all this most clearly, but not even he was able to convince the British churches of the vital part played by the arts in the communication of religious truth.

One area of the visual arts field into which all the churches have entered in considerable force during the past quarter of a century is that occupied by architecture. The massive movement and growth of population which has characterized the post-World War II years has perforce driven the churches to erect many new buildings. Millions of pounds have been raised for this purpose and there is no urban area in the country which does not have one or more new buildings. It would be pleasant to record that these buildings now stand as powerful testimonies to the truths of the gospel and as enhancements of the environments

103

in which they are located. In fact, the overwhelming majority of them fail on both counts. The normal post-war church building is as uninspiring as it is theologically misleading, though it may be argued with some plausibility that the buildings reflect with a high degree of accuracy the lack of vision and confusion about the nature of the church which has characterized the era in which they were erected.

Space will not permit a detailed consideration of the actual results of this tragic failure, but examples will be found within walking distance of the homes of most of the readers of this book and may be examined at first hand. Inadequate ground plans, unimaginative and inefficient use of space, and tawdry furnishings are the order of the day. Even Coventry Cathedral, held up as Britain's great contribution to contemporary church architecture, must be accounted a miserable failure, notwithstanding the fact that it houses some very fine works of art. Significantly, the excellent work carried out by the cathedral staff over the past decade has served only to emphasize the inadequacy of the liturgical base from which they have been operating. The building came into its own for a short period in 1968 when the Bishop of Coventry, disregarding the advice of the cathedral staff, used it for a nineteenth-century style mission at which he and other evangelists harangued well-marshalled multitudes.

A church building should stand as a visual statement about the nature of the Christian gospel and the character of the Christian community. The mediaeval buildings offered such a statement with great clarity, both externally and internally. We may no longer care for the theological insights they portray, but because they represented deeply held convictions and were erected to serve a well-defined function they still stand in many English towns and villages as rich examples of architectural art and retain their power to inspire. The fact that we no longer think of transcendence in the same way as our forefathers in the fourteenth century, nor face the world equipped with a monumental Thomist theology, nor enjoy a dominating role in society, does not mean that contemporary church buildings need be any less artistic or less inspiring. They will obviously be different from the churches we have inherited from the past, but there is no reason why they should be inferior in either appearance or functional utility. Examples of modern church building in Europe and North America prove this conclusively.

The servant character of the church, which may be regarded as perhaps the dominant insight of the modern theologian, and is combined with a revived appreciation of God's immanence, can be represented in visual architectural terms with great effect, once it is recognized that servanthood is not to be confused with servitude and that God's immanence does not necessarily involve the substitution of table-tennis tables for Communion tables. It may be argued that during the past twenty-five years Britain has been extremely short of visionary architects, and the standard of public building generally (with the notable exception of schools in certain parts of the country) offers strong support for this argument. But the tragedy of church architecture in this period cannot be blamed on the architects. Within the churches themselves there has been an obstinate refusal to recognize the visual importance of buildings and a persistent unwillingness to ask the primary question: what is this building for and how best will it serve the needs of those who will use it? Had this question not been brushed aside and had a tiny proportion of the total sum of money spent on building been devoted to research – involving theologians, architects, sociologists and members of local churches – the emergence of a new school of church architects might well have been the result and future generations would then have been able to look back on the 1950s and 1960s with gratitude.

Here, once again, is an instance of what happens in the field of Christian communication when the highest priority is given to the verbal, and the visual is almost totally neglected. Fortunately there is now a glimmer of hope on the horizon in the emergence of Birmingham University's Institute for the Study of Worship and Religious Architecture. The small, but highly competent, staff of the Institute are forcing some of the fundamental questions upon the churches and offering the fruits of their own researches in this country and in Europe. But the resources available to the Institute are ridiculously small in relation to the need and efforts to persuade the churches that a modest investment in this establishment would pay handsome dividends have not been successful. Financial pressures are now beginning to restrict the number of church building projects in most parts of the country and the advance of the ecumenical movement may well lead to a reduction in the number of church buildings in many communities. Some post-war buildings are already redundant. But a massive task of re-ordering the interiors of the existing churches is waiting to be carried out, and until significant progress has been made here most of our churches will not only be inconvenient to use but also present in a powerful visual form a false impression of what the Christian community is meant to be and what its relations with the outside world ought to be in process of becoming. The finest sermons and the most competent educational programmes are quickly neutralized by an unsatisfactory church interior, for the eye is more sensitive than the ear and the impressions it receives are always likely to last longer.

# 7 The Church is the Message

The main theme of this book so far has been that the church, the community of faith, is under compulsion to communicate its insights into the nature of the kingdom of God to those who have not yet received them. We have seen that this compulsion derives not from obedience to a divine fiat but from a burning desire to share with others something which the individual Christian and the community to which he belongs finds uniquely precious. Underlying this basic theme is a personal conviction that over the course of the centuries – more particularly the recent centuries – there has been an excessive emphasis on verbalizing the Christian gospel. In consequence, a wide variety of channels of communication have been neglected. This neglect is now in urgent need of repair, not least because of the new insights into the nature of communication and the new techniques of communication which have become available in the present century. If the church exists primarily as a communications centre it can hardly afford to ignore any of the effective means of sharing information, insight and experience now to hand as a result of advances in human knowledge during the past fifty years. All the evidence suggests that we are now only at the beginning of a communications explosion which is destined to transform the whole environment in which men and communities relate to one another. Hence the need for the churches to take much more seriously the techniques of communication and be prepared to redeploy its resources of manpower and money so that these techniques may be more efficiently exploited.

In order to avoid serious misunderstanding, I feel compelled to emphasize as strongly as possible that the effective use of modern techniques of communication will not necessarily lead to a wider acceptance of the Christian insight nor an increase in the size of the church's membership. After all, the church is not selling soap. The Christian gospel offers liberation and the possibility of living life to the full, but it also makes considerable demands. The way to resurrection is through the cross and there are many reasons why individuals are unable to accept its demands. If the life and ministry of Jesus offers a model for the church in every age, there is every reason for supposing that the number of those who can receive the gospel in its fulness will always be relatively small. This being so, it may well be that the more effective communication of the gospel will lead to a diminution of the number of people who describe themselves as Christians and who are ready to identify themselves with the church. In many parts of the western world the prevailing expressions of the Christian faith represent serious distortions of the message of Jesus, and commitment to the church is based on social, psychological and conventional demands. In such a situation a clear communication of the gospel might have a devastating effect upon the existing church communities. One cannot be sure about this. There is no necessary virtue in having a minority role and it is dangerous to seek one. But it is of quite fundamental importance to recognize that 'success' in the field of Christian communication may well be expressed differently from 'success' in other communication enterprises.

Having recognized the need to exploit every available form of communication, especially those employing non-verbal methods, and having recognized that the results of our efforts may not be precisely what we anticipate or desire, we are now brought face to face with a fact which is simple, yet devastating in its implications and demands. *The church itself is the primary means of Christian communication.*

The biblical basis of this statement need not be expounded at length. The Old Testament story is of a God who acts in the world, and reveals his will and purpose for humanity, through a community of people. Within that community there were individuals who had a good deal to say about many different things. But they spoke within a community and to a community. The prophets did not address themselves to mankind in general or offer ready-made solutions to world problems. Their message was to the Israelite nation – the People of God – and the purpose of their words and deeds was to call the nation to fulfil its calling in the world, which was to exemplify all that was involved in living under the sovereignty of God. They were to disclose in concrete terms, in the day-to-day life of human communities, how life was to be lived in all its fulness and all its glory.

Just why God chose to communicate with the human race in this way can only be a matter for speculation. But, given the nature of the world, the character of man and God's unceasing involvement within his creation, the choice of a group of people to serve as a channel of communication does at least indicate a degree of consistency. Although man is capable of abstract thought and has created models of the universe which suggest that the world is but a shadow of a more fundamental expression of reality, he is essentially an earthy being whose life is dominated by the fulfilment of present, concrete needs. Attempts to communicate with him at any other level have never been successful, nor can they be successful since man's nature is not abstract but real. Meaningful expressions of religious insight and experience must, therefore, be clothed in the form which is natural to man, and the genius of the Hebrew/Christian religion lies in its recognition of this fundamental truth.

Hence the divine disclosure, not through complex systems of thought or the movement of the planets, but through the lives of individual men and women and through the life of a particular community. The demand of the present generation of young people, 'Don't tell me; show me', is not new. It has been the unceasing cry of humanity since the dawn of history. We cannot order our lives satisfactorily in response to commands, advice or exhortation; we need to have set before us concrete expressions of wisdom and love to which we can relate in intimate terms.

The vocation of the Israelite people was to provide such a concrete expression, in order that God's loving purposes might be disclosed, and the Old Testament is essentially the story of a struggle to perfect communication between God and man. That failure and frustration occupies so prominent a part in this story should not blind us to what was actually taking place nor to the extent to which the reality of man's relations with God and his fellows was actually expressed. Comparison with any other contemporary religion shows just how much the human race as a whole owes to the Jews for the insights which have been received into the nature and destiny of man through their co-operation with the divine will. The Old Testament prophets had ample scope for denunciation, since there was much that was imperfect in the life of the Israelite community, but even so the history of Israel offered, and still offers, a concrete example of the creative effect of man's response to the love of God.

It is against this background that the life and work of Jesus is to be evaluated. The incarnation involved no radically new approach by God in his dealings with men. The loving purpose which controls the life of the world, and is expressed in the life of every human being, was again revealed in terms which could be seen, experienced and assimilated by those who came into contact with a particular man – Jesus of Nazareth. 'The Word was made flesh.' Wherein lay the distinction of Jesus from those who were his followers or who lived in Nazareth and Jerusalem during the same period of history? Certainly not in any physical or mental dissimilarity, for he was a real human being and subject to the same limitations as his contemporaries. The uniqueness of Jesus lay in the fact that in him the love which belongs to the nature and being of God, and which occupies the central position in the life of every human being, found perfect expression, thus revealing in a uniquely powerful way what man truly is – and is capable of becoming.

The essential humanity of Jesus is quite crucial at this point. Once he is removed in Christian thought from the human scene and placed in a special category which suggests a role analogous to that of a divine 'invader', the possibility of communication disappears from view. It is precisely because Jesus was 'like as we are' that we are able to receive from him a supreme revelation about our own nature. This emphasis upon the humanity of Jesus in no way denies his divinity, since the love of God was

110

manifestly and uniquely disclosed in his life. It does, however, emphasize the essentially divine character of *every* human being. We are all sons of God, and the Christian life consists in allowing this fact to find expression in concrete action after the pattern set by Jesus.

To those seeking to follow this pattern, the words of Jesus as contained in the New Testament are precious. His parables and preaching and sayings bring us into touch with the truth. As we reflect upon them, we see into the reality of our own nature and that of mankind as a whole. But more important than the words of Jesus – which we may or may not have in the form in which they were originally uttered – is the life which gave expression to these words. It is as we catch glimpses of a life in which love was expressed in deep concern for others, ranging from the innocent child to the corrupted prostitute, that we discover who we really are and what kind of a person we might become. Supremely this is revealed in the crucifixion where we see love expressed in the clearest and most powerful form that man is capable of receiving. So the focus of the Christian revelation is not a saying but a cross; the central Christian response to that revelation is not obedience to a codified ethic but the sharing in a community meal. It is through the life and death of Jesus that the essential communication of love takes place and the gateway to resurrection is opened.

Nearly 2000 years of Christian history have served to confirm this basic truth. Such evidence of the life of the earliest Christian communities as can be extracted from the New Testament shows that the followers of Jesus endeavoured to share their experience with others by means of the spoken word, while the epistles provide examples of the employment of the written word. But the overwhelming impression is given that those attracted into membership of the church were more powerfully influenced by the quality of love exhibited within the Christian community than by the eloquence of the apostolic preachers. Hence Paul's great concern for the right ordering of the life of the churches which he had founded. Some of the details of his letters may not seem directly relevant to the life of the church today, nor is there any reason why they should provide precise guidelines for the church of the twentieth century, but they indicate Paul's deep, and significant, awareness that the life of the Christian community must be an accurate reflection of character of the gospel. Neither powerful preaching nor sensational miracles could take the place of the divine love expressed through the relationships which existed amongst those who constituted the community of Christ.

So it has always been down the centuries. The Christian faith has never been effectively communicated by a corrupt church. There have been periods in history when the church has produced monumental buildings and theologies. There have been times when the church has exercised extensive temporal power and taken possession of the consciences of individuals. But, on the whole, these have not been eras of effective Christian communication. It is when the love of God has been revealed in the lives of individual men and women, and in the life of the church itself, that the world has been moved to enquire whether the Christian gospel might have light to throw upon the human condition.

The same is true today. In the final resort men and women will be attracted to a place within range of the Christian gospel not by means of the techniques of persuasion but by the quality of life they see exhibited by those who claim to be under the influence of the divine love. Pronouncements, public relations exercises, sophisticated broadcasting techniques and so forth will serve little purpose unless the life of the Christian community is a living and dynamic expression of love. The only effective visual aid and channel of Christian communication is the life of the local church.

Hence the need for constant examination of the life of the church to ensure that it reflects with some degree of accuracy that which it exists to experience and communicate. Perfection will, of course, never be achieved. The forces opposed to love are at work in every human being and in every institution. The church may expect to have its share of them, and no programme of reform and renewal which does not take account of this fact will ever achieve anything. Like St Paul, we may hope for a church which is 'without spot or wrinkle or any such thing', as indeed we expect to find in every Christian the clear marks of sanctity. But the Christian hope is eschatological, and perfection must await the end of history.

In the meantime, there is normally enough to be getting on with to secure the reform of Christian individuals and communities, and especially at the present time when the Christian faith is facing the new challenges of a rapidly changing world. Without falling into the trap of introversion, the question must continually be asked: 'Does the life of the church in this place adequately reflect, and therefore communicate, the heart of the gospel?'

Implicit in this question is the conviction that the local church still has a crucial part to play in the service of the kingdom of God. This is not to say that what happens within the church at the national and international levels is unimportant. If, for instance, the Vatican appears in the eyes of the world as an inhuman, devious and corrupt instrument of ecclesiastical government, the credibility of the gospel is bound to be called in question by many thoughtful people. Or if the actions of the Church of England's General Synod appear to be trivial, partisan and unrelated to anything that touches the lives of normal men and women, it will not be surprising if there are those who wonder whether the recognition of the centrality of love in human experience has any meaning and value. Having spent several years in the press seats at assemblies representing almost every level of the life of the church, I am bound to record my thankfulness that such gatherings are rarely observed by the general public. If it were otherwise, the damage to the Christian cause would be incalculable. Much remains to be done before any of the churches can begin to communicate the gospel at this important point in their corporate lives.

Again, emphasis on the crucial place of the local church does not imply backing for the parochial system as presently worked in the Church of England and, in a slightly modified form, in the other churches. The word 'local' has taken on an entirely new meaning in the twentieth century. In earlier times, when people lived and worked in the same neighbourhood, it was possible to define locality in fairly precise geographical terms. Most of the villages and small towns were virtually self-contained and, though they were related somewhat tenuously to other communities, they had a recognizably organic life of their own. This is no longer the case, except in a decreasing number of places remote from metropolitan influence. Locality, for many people, is now experienced in terms of an industrial complex, a comprehensive school or a region which provides them with a variety of interests spread over a wide area. The places where individuals actually reside are becoming less and less important as centres of activity and influence, though it would be wrong to dismiss them as being of no importance in the creation of community.

In whatever sphere, then, the church is required to operate it is to be a communications centre for the kingdom of God and it will carry out this function by developing a four-fold action programme.

1. *A centre of proclamation*   Although the church is not to be equated with the kingdom of God and shares common ground with all who are seeking to improve the lot of mankind, it does have certain distinctive insights and experiences which it feels impelled to share with all who are prepared to listen. A large part of this book has been occupied with discussing the many different ways in which insight and experience may be shared. It only remains for me to plead that this aspect of the church's work be not further neglected. Not every church community has the same resources available to it. Some are more fortunate than others in their reserves of skill and money. But it ought surely to be possible for an intelligent enquirer to discover from his local church what life in the kingdom of God involves and on what intellectual base it is built. This raises some important questions concerning the role of clergy and ministers.

Enough has, I hope, been said to indicate that the ordained man has no monopoly of the truth, theological or otherwise. The reflective layman has insight to offer and is nearly always better able to communicate theology in terms which other laymen can understand. If, however, laymen are to become theologians and develop their skills they will normally need encouragement and also an opportunity to share their reflections with others. It is at this point that the clergyman can offer his own resources. All being well, he will have had three or four years of full-time academic study and, although much of what he was taught is not directly relevant either to his own experience or that of any other living human being, he should have learned the art of disciplined thought and a good deal about the experience of Christians across the centuries. If he has attended a fairly reasonable college, he may even have discovered something about the thought of contemporary theologians. And if he has the time, money and inclination he will have kept up to date with current developments. None of this can be a substitute for the working out of a personal, existential theology, but it is an invaluable resource for a local church which, as a community, is trying to present to a neighbourhood or social grouping an approach to the kingdom of God which makes it possible for a modern man to make the leap of faith without denying his intellectual integrity.

This is the primary role of the full-time clergyman. It is quite unnecessary to have a rigorous theological education in order to administer the sacraments. Training in psychology and social work can, of course, help a man to be a better pastor, but since few ministers have ever had such training there is no reason for them to assume complete responsibility for the pastoral work of a neighbourhood. The church of the not-too-distant future is more than likely to be using auxiliary or non-professional ministers for both these functions. But there remains, and will continue to remain, a special role for the man who has had the necessary training – and, equally important, is allowed the time – to enable him to engage in theological reflection. It may not be possible for every local church to have the full-time services of such a man, but groups of churches should be able to share one and it is of the utmost importance that these men should have the necessary intellectual gifts and be skilled in communication. All the signs indicate that the church is to be required to proclaim the gospel within a context in which serious intellectual questions demand serious intellectual answers. There is no reason why the church should be afraid of this development. On the contrary it is something to be welcomed, for Christians believe that it is the truth that sets men free. And it is possible to put up as reasonable an intellectual case for the Christian faith as it is for any other philosophy of life. In this situation, however, it is better to have fewer, better-equipped, full-time clerics than the present army of men recruited to provide general purpose leadership for thousands of local units. The standard to be aimed at should be such as to enable there to be an easy interchange between those serving as local church theologians and those serving as teachers in colleges and seminaries. The possibility of interchange would do much to transform the character of the theological education at present offered in the colleges.

Every local church must become a theological centre with its own resources, constantly renewed, for communicating the truth concerning the kingdom of God, and within reach of special resources which may be required to meet special needs. The religious orders could be of considerable assistance to the church here, and though it is not necessary for every bishop and church leader to be recruited from an academic sphere, the intellectual calibre and reflective ability of candidates for positions of leadership in the church should become a much more important factor than appears to have been the case in the recent past. A church which fails to take theology seriously is doomed.

2. *A centre of reconciliation*   The kingdom of God is the realm in which love, acceptance and peace reign supreme. Christians believe that reconciliation between man and God involves reconciliation between man and man. This truth must therefore be reflected and expressed in the life of the local church. Here is the place where the barriers which divide people and create destructive tensions must be broken down. It seems hardly necessary to catalogue the points at which tension is being experienced in modern society, so pressing are the crises we now face. The racial barrier in Britain is no lower than it was a decade ago. Indeed, thanks to the efforts of men like Mr Enoch Powell (himself a professed Anglican), the situation has in many places deteriorated. It is not fair to lay at the door of every local church blame for the fact that, even in areas of high immigration, the number of black people in the congregation is small. There are

cultural and traditional factors which often make it difficult for people from other lands to feel at home in the milieu of British churches, even when the local Christians are friendly, hospitable and non-patronizing in their approach to visitors from abroad. Even so, there are few places where local churches might not make a greatly increased effort to provide facilities for people of differing races to meet and thus begin to break down the barriers which keep them apart.

Another area of tension concerns the barrier between rich and poor. Although the achievements of the welfare state have been remarkable, the fact remains (though it is normally overlooked or disbelieved) that the gap between the financial position of the rich and the poor has widened, and is still widening. The Anglican and Free Churches in Britain draw their membership largely from the better-off members of society. The reasons for this go back to the nineteenth century, as do those which give the Roman Catholic Church a predominantly artisan membership. Such long-standing developments are not easily reversed, but it is surely impossible for the followers of the poor man of Nazareth to sit at ease while their neighbours in the pews are drawn almost exclusively from those fortunate enough to occupy positions in the upper income bracket. Closely related to this is the barrier between management and workers in industry which, in spite of modest improvements in industrial relations during the past twenty-five years, remains a major obstacle to the unity of the British nation. Once again it has to be acknowledged that the church's membership tends to be drawn almost exclusively from the managerial and professional classes, thus reflecting the polarization which exists in society and making little contribution towards the creation of a local or national community in which brotherhood and equality are the controlling factors.

Some of the most constructive work here is being carried out by the industrial missions. Developing from the pioneering work of Ted Wickham in Sheffield in 1944, there are now more than 200 industrial chaplains working in various parts of Britain and, though the extent and quality of their work is far from uniform, the contribution of the industrial missions has been one of the

117

most encouraging features of the church scene in Britain during the past quarter of a century. The Teesside Industrial Mission, for example, employs nine full-time chaplains and has built up a wide network of contacts over a key area in North-East England. Under its auspices, managers and shop stewards have been brought together to discuss their particular and common problems in an atmosphere quite different from that which exists at the negotiating table. Foremen have been able to articulate the acute tension which dominates their lives as they are subjected to pressure from both sides of industry. The human factors involved in redundancy and re-training have been brought into the open and policies modified to meet human needs. The Teesside chaplains would be the first to admit that their contribution to the solution of massive problems has been modest, yet it remains highly significant and points the way forward for a church which communicates the gospel by exercising a reconciling function in society.

Yet another barrier awaiting destruction is that which divides the sexes and consigns women to a subordinate role in society. The Women's Liberation Movement – sometimes driven by frustration to extreme tactics – is always good for a joke or a wisecrack, yet represents a necessary rebellion against a social structure which has for centuries dehumanized one half of society. This is not the place to discuss the implications of discrimination against women, or the future role of women, but if the church exists to be a reconciling agency in which 'there is neither Jew nor Gentile, male nor female, bond nor free' we cannot avoid asking why the church has not been in the forefront of the movement for the emancipation of women? And, having asked the question, one is obliged to face the unpleasant truth that, far from leading the way, the church has in fact been a powerful force in restricting the sphere of female activity and may well be the last social institution in which they are permitted to exercise responsibility.

If, for instance, I suggest that by the end of the century a woman may be the Pope or the Archbishop of Canterbury most people will tell me that I am being unrealistic, which is doubtless true.

But some Christians will tell me that I have ventured into the realm of the unthinkable – or even the obscene. At the local church level the number of women holding office as church-wardens, society stewards, secretaries and treasurers is increasing, but remains very small. The mere suggestion that they should assume such offices is sufficient to cause deep controversy in most places. There are, of course, very few ordained women in Britain, nor are there likely to be many during the remaining years of this century. The reasons for this situation are well known and need not be rehearsed. Conservatism rather than anti-feminism is the primary factor. But, whatever the reason, the restriction of women to positions outside the leadership of the churches is a flagrant denial of the true nature of the Christian community and, therefore, a barrier to the communication of the gospel.

Until the local churches have begun to attack these – and other – barriers with energy, imagination and skill, the world is going to experience the greatest difficulty in hearing that gospel of the kingdom of God which the Christian community exists to communicate. No amount of advanced television technique or compelling literature will compensate for failure at this point.

3. *A centre for the underprivileged* A distinctive feature of the ministry of Jesus was his concern for the underprivileged, of whom there were a great many in the society in which he lived. This concern sprang from his love of individuals which went out most powerfully to those in greatest need. It was also a living proclamation of the kingdom of God in which the love of God for all his people is expressed in the acceptance and care which leads to an enhancement of human life. If, therefore, the church is to communicate the gospel it, too, must be concerned with the enhancement of human life at every level – with marked emphasis on the physical elements necessary to happiness.

The western world of the twentieth century has made remark-able progress in alleviating the worst pains of disease and poverty, yet there remain many areas of life in which neglect is normal. The chances of securing adequate treatment for acute mental illness are remote. The conditions in prisons are inhuman and the provisions for prison after-care totally inadequate. Elderly people are kept from the risk of starvation but also from the opportunity of comfort. Those – young and old – who cannot adjust to the present patterns of society and turn to the streets of our anonymous cities in a desperate attempt to escape from its demands are offered little assistance. The disabled are required to face not only the pain and restrictions of their disability but also punitive financial penalties.

These, and many other, examples of deprivation indicate clearly that there are still a very considerable number of people, even in the most highly privileged nations of the world, who are experiencing acute suffering and not living their lives to the full potential. The scope for the churches is, therefore, unlimited and though it is important that individual Christians should be encouraged to assist in improving the human lot through involvement in the work of the statutory and voluntary social services, and that local churches should be ready to co-operate with these services, there will, within the foreseeable future, remain areas of human need which are hardly likely to be tackled unless the church assumes responsibility or gives a lead in the community. Before doing this, however, the churches might well consider how far their own community life is open to the underprivileged. The physically handicapped, for example: does the church building have a wide enough door, and possibly a ramp, to facilitate the entry of those who are confined to invalid chairs? Are those who are seriously handicapped encouraged to hold office in a local church or is it simply taken for granted that they are generally incapable or may not be able to attend meetings? What attempts are made to engage those with psychological disorders in the life of the church community where love and acceptance can often work greater miracles than drugs or analysis? How much of the church budget is set aside for the financial support of individuals and families in need?

These are just a few of the areas of human need which a church sensitive to the existence of the underprivileged might attempt to meet and, in so doing, express its understanding of the gospel. But the underprivileged in our society not only require assistance in tackling immediate, particular needs. They need a mouthpiece through which their feelings of deprivation may be voiced and brought to the attention of the wider community. Democracy is still a long way from perfection. These are the days of the big battalions, and minority groups tend to be heard and neglected – especially if they make inconvenient demands on those who are enjoying comfort and security. We have yet to devise means by which the voice of the little man can be heard, and the church is never going to be in a position to solve this problem. Yet the church has both the strength and the freedom to make a very significant contribution at this point. In every locality in Britain it has a permanent platform. Its leaders are still able to command the attention of the mass media, and would in fact receive even more attention if their utterances and actions were related to real human issues. Some ecclesiastics still walk in the corridors of power.

If the image of the church suggested that one of its primary concerns was with improving the lot of the underprivileged members of society, it would doubtless lose a good deal of 'respectable' support and make plenty of enemies. But this would be a small price to pay for the fulfilment of its role as a sign and a servant of the kingdom of God and, therefore, a centre for the communication of the gospel.

4. *A centre of celebration*   One of my favourite stories about St Martin-in-the-Fields concerns a man who attended the church during the remarkable ministry of Dick Sheppard. He had just been discharged from the nearby Charing Cross Hospital after undergoing an operation for the removal of his appendix, but quickly had to be re-admitted for so great was his laughter during the service at St Martin's that the surgeon's stitches were broken! Church communities are not, however, normally recognized as places of jollification and fun. On the contrary, they usually give the impression of unrelieved gloom or, at least, of extreme formality.

More often than not, church buildings are dimly lit and un-attractively adorned, in contrast to the mediaeval edifices which were usually a riot of colour and uplifting to the spirit through their form and atmosphere. Again, Christian worship is rarely exciting and stimulating; normally it is doleful, predictable and, for many, extremely depressing. The arrangement of furnishings is such as to encourage formality and discourage real encounter. A church building is one of the few places of human assembly where it is difficult to relax and where individuals go in fear of falling out of step.

Yet the Christian faith is supposed to value joy as one of the cardinal virtues. The kingdom of God provides the secret of life and points the way to human fulfilment. Through anticipation of the resurrection and the heavenly banquet, the church on earth banishes gloom and despondency and engages in a continuous round of celebration. Here is a community of people who are not weighted down by the cares and contradictions of ordinary human existence. And it cannot be doubted that the modern world desperately needs to be informed and influenced by such a community. In spite of the fact that the machine is removing much of the drudgery from life and promises to release mankind for enjoyment and creative leisure, there are as yet few signs of joy on the human scene. On the contrary, the contents of radio or television news bulletins are such as to encourage suicide and the unceasing search for new forms of amusement is a symptom of a society which has lost the art of celebration through the centuries of submission to puritan doctrines of work. The hippy who chooses to spend his days in a park in the company of a few guitar-playing friends, rather than submit to the demands of industry or commerce, reflects a basically healthy reaction against a pernicious form of enslavement.

Now, of course, the Christian concept of the kingdom of God does not suggest that life is one long round of fun and high jinks. Experience teaches otherwise. Neither does an external smile necessarily reflect interior joy. Again, it is to be recognized that there are solemn forms of celebration. A symphony concert may be a more profound expression of celebration than a boisterous party at which the wine flows freely and paper hats are compulsory. Yet, having acknowledged all this, it is impossible to doubt that most of our local churches will need a major revolution before they can be described as centres of celebration without the risk of a prosecution under the Trade Descriptions Act. Paint brushes, a more catholic approach to music, greater flexibility in the ordering of worship, readiness to move furniture, freedom to express (rather than repress) feelings, recognition of the virtues of informality, liberation from the fear of making mistakes; these are some of the ingredients necessary for the creation of communities of celebration.

It would be absurd to pretend that changes in this direction are likely to be easy, or would be warmly welcomed by those who now attend the worship in local churches. Long years of history and tradition are not wiped away overnight and the churches need protection against wild young ministers who believe that guitars, drums and streamers will solve every theological and liturgical problem. But a firm movement towards the conversion of local churches into centres of celebration is long overdue and there are signs that the insight and material necessary for this process is now becoming available.

In case the point has not been made with sufficient clarity, I emphasize that the aim here is not to attract more people into church buildings – or even to convert them to the Christian faith – by the use of new techniques. The aim is simply to make local church communities into more vivid expressions of life in the kingdom of God and, therefore, more effective communicators of the gospel.

Those involved in the leadership of local churches will, perhaps, nod their heads in approval at this point (some with greater vigour than others) but then explode into anger born of frustration because it seems impossible to translate this four-fold programme into action in the situation in which they now find themselves. It is one thing to produce a blue-print in a book; quite another to turn it into reality when resources are small, tradition firmly entrenched and every available minute and ounce of energy required to keep the existing church community alive. Since this is the situation of so many clergy, ministers and active laymen, is it not highly irresponsible to write a book which suggests various courses of action which, while obviously highly desirable in themselves, are impossible of realization and therefore fuel for increased frustration?

The question is a fair one and cannot be ignored. No one who is in touch with those responsible for the leadership of local churches, particularly in the inner-city areas or remote rural districts, can have anything but the utmost sympathy for the agony which many of them are suffering through their impotence in the face of apparently immoveable ecclesiastical structures. Unless the situation is changed within the near future it would be reasonable to expect an increase in the number of breakdowns among the clergy and in the number of those who retreat into inaction or find fulfilment elsewhere.

There appear to be only two ways out of this situation and their acceptance and implementation is now a matter of extreme urgency. Opinions may differ about precise detail, so I will concentrate on broad principles and emphasize these with as much conviction as I can now muster, leaving others to work out the implications in their own situations.

The first involves the ecumenical movement. After nearly twenty years of negotiation designed to unite particular churches, it has become fashionable to declare ecumenical ideals redundant. Where this springs from impatience with the lack of progress in top-level discussions it is perfectly understandable, though profoundly mistaken. The unification of churches is still urgently necessary because it is impossible for them to communicate that concept of reconciliation which is fundamental to any understanding of the kingdom of God while they are still divided. It is also impossible for them to mount the resources needed for mission in today's world while so much money, so much ministerial manpower and so many buildings are deployed wastefully.

With the exception of rural areas, there are few parts of Britain where a very considerable saving of money could not be effected by the bringing together of one or more congregations in a single building. Current expenditure on the lighting, heating and maintenance of unnecessary buildings has now reached scandalous proportions and prevents the development of new work. Clergy and ministers working in isolation, and frequently overlapping in pastoral responsibilities, are less effective than teams in which individuals can develop particular gifts and provide

124

mutual support. The division of a decreasing number of active laity into separate congregations is weakening and demoralizing.

All this is well known and requires no elaboration here. I simply point out that the implementation of the four-point programme discussed earlier in this chapter will, in many places, depend on the local churches being prepared to pool their resources and insights. Those who are frustrated by the present inability of their churches to communicate the truth concerning the kingdom of God in their neighbourhood may reflect with profit on the fact that, while God provides the church with resources sufficient for its witness in the world, he does not offer a bounty sufficient to support the luxury of the church's present divisions.

The second principle is rather more radical. Where a local church is unable to function effectively as a centre of proclamation, reconciliation, concern for the underprivileged and celebration, it should cease to exist. Many of the present units of local church life are hindrances to the advancement of the kingdom of God because, far from communicating its insights to the neighbourhood, they present a totally false picture of what life in the kingdom involves. Every local church is, for better or for worse, a communications centre. The important question is: what is this community communicating – either by intention or by default?

It would be infinitely preferable to have fewer, but more effective, centres of Christian communication than the present multitude of local churches, many of which cannot sustain a credible witness. Such a reduction in numbers would not necessarily lead to a withdrawal from areas of present influence since it is reasonable to suppose that strong and effective churches would quickly find appropriate ways of permeating the districts for which they were responsible. It is remarkable how quickly and how widely a church becomes known when it begins to meet real human need.

Actions speak louder than words. This is an old saying and has lost much of its power through constant repetition. But it remains true for mankind as a whole, and not least for the Christian church. For nearly two thousand years the teaching of Jesus has been transmitted across the generations and to every part of the world. Innumerable sermons have been preached extolling the virtues of the gospel. Countless books have been written to explain what Jesus really meant. And in every age there have been groups of people whose lives have displayed the beauty and glory of life in the kingdom of God. It is to these groups that we owe most, and if the good news is to be conveyed to those whose lives will be spent mainly in the twenty-first century, it will be because the church today recognizes more clearly that the eye is more important than the ear and that the re-ordering of its corporate life at every level is now more important than the reinterpretation of its theology.